Happy Valley Hockey

BEN JONES

© 2017 Ben Jones
All rights reserved.

ISBN: 0692964037
ISBN 13: 9780692964033

FOREWORD

The 1,500-mile Appalachian Mountain range envelops the commonwealth of Pennsylvania, making it one of the more beautiful and awe-inspiring states in the U.S. There is plenty of room with plenty of views. The highways wind, dip and ascend. The vistas are equal parts intimidating, breathtaking and majestic -- a scenic contributor to our beautiful continent.

Smack dab in the middle of Pennsylvania, 1,200 feet above sea level in the Allegheny Mountain section of the Appalachians, is the campus of Penn State University. Although located in a part of the state with so much room, Penn State (the library, residence halls, athletic fields and venues et al) is packed into State College like a meaty hoagie.

There were 851 people in State College at the turn of 19th century. When the 20th century became the 21st, the number was 38,000. The tiny town became a large town because of Penn State, and that's what it is today: a large small town with a very large school.

I first heard of Penn State's interest in becoming a big-time NCAA hockey program while covering the 2010 Stanley Cup finals for ESPN between the Philadelphia Flyers and Chicago Blackhawks.

I was told at a Chicago steakhouse that there was a rich man named Terry Pegula, a Penn State alum, who was about to become storybook wealthy. At the time, Pegula was closing out the sale of the company he founded called East Resources, a natural gas drilling company. The sale price was $4.7 billion. That's billions with a 'b'.

The story of the Penn State donation began in 2005, when Pegula had dinner with Joe Battista, the club hockey coach at Penn State, at Kelly's Steak and Seafood just outside State College. Pegula asked Battista, "Joe, why can't we play Michigan, Notre Dame and Ohio State in hockey? Why can't we have big-time college hockey at Penn State?"

In the end, when all was said, done, and built, the final financial gift Terry and Kim Pegula would give the university to instantly have a first-class, five-star college hockey program was more than $100 million, the largest private gift in Penn State history. An angel had descended upon State College for those who love hockey and for those looking for a fresh chapter in Penn State's tainted history.

I was at Pegula Ice Arena and broadcasting the game when Penn State's earned its first Big Ten victory. The Nittany Lions got their first conference win after nine tries, a 4-0 victory over Michigan on a Saturday on ESPNU in 2014 in front a standing-room-only crowd of 6,170. Baby steps.

Getting that first Big Ten win in school history was so important. Hockey is hard. Losing a lot in hockey can make it unbearably demanding. It was just Penn State's second win over a two month period. As if winter in Central Pennsylvania isn't trying enough. As if those towering Pennsylvania mountains aren't punishing enough to climb.

But with each win, you learn, move on, build, get better, hope, and dream. You never stop climbing the mountain. Penn State is here for good, striving every day toward the green summit of a National Championship. This is story at how they arrived so quickly at the base of that mountain. A story where almost every decision was the correct one.

John Buccigross August 2017

"And for the team, I always tried to do the right thing"
Steve Yzerman

Happy Valley Hockey

41.6113° N, 79.6584° W

By 1859, life had taken its toll on Edwin Drake and the bags below his eyes told a story of misfortunes and trials, a life that felt far longer than it had truly been. Born in Greenville, NY some 40 years prior it was not long before Drake set out on his own. His time was spent between his family's two farms, one in New York and another in Vermont. He was accustomed to a life of travel.

Perhaps it was only natural that he found himself working his way up the ladder to the role of conductor in New Haven, Connecticut, riding trains to and from stops, the world blowing on by through the New England sun. But a summer illness would rob Drake of his job, and in 1854 the birth of his second child would rob him of his wife. With little education Drake was on the edge, with little purpose and even fewer options.

Fortunately for Drake, his status as a former conductor allowed him to keep the benefit of free travel, one of the few constants in his life. That travel would eventually bring him, his new wife, and children to a city that much like Drake, was looking for its meaning. To Titusville, Pa.

Drake would find that meaning at Seneca Oil Company which hired him to search for potential oil deposits in Titusville. The search was, like so many things in Drake's life, a struggle. He persevered, carrying on with the drilling, looking for something he might not find with a process that might not work.

And then 69.5 feet below the surface he found what he was looking for. The first American oil well was born, and with it a revolution that would change a nation and shape a world. Drake and his counterparts did not know that they sat atop one of the richest areas of natural gas and oil in the entire country. The technology to find it and take it from the Earth was still decades down the road, but it was there all the same.

If we were to enter a time machine and to travel roughly 387 million years into the past the hints would have been there. Then again, Drake would have found himself below the surface of an ocean that covered much of Western PA and the better part of West Virginia and lower New York.

Eventually those waters would recede as the planet changed. That ocean left behind a clay and sand rock that is compacted and pressed together into its final form, shale. Given the long passage of time and calm waters, shale became a common sedimentary rock throughout the region.

Shale itself is a fairly common. It's found in large quantities across nearly every continent including some regions in Africa. What makes this particular shale region so special, is shale gas, or in laymen's terms, gas trapped within the layers of shale. The Marcellus Shale we call it now.

Getting to it was a skill that would take nearly another 150 years to hone, but it was just six years following Drake's well before Col. Edward A.L Roberts of Virginia designed a technique that would later enable modern fracking in 1865, even if he didn't know it at the time.

History refers to it as U.S. Patent No. 59,936 a fairly nondescript title for a technique that would help change the world some day. In more straightforward terms, Roberts had devised a system that in essence dropped a torpedo down an oil well, attempting to force cracks and openings that would in turn create access to more oil.

It didn't take long for Roberts to run into issues. He invented fluid tamping, a process by which sand and water is poured into the well prior to detonation. The mixture would then enter the natural cracks and the ensuing explosion would force it to break far more effectively. While the true benefits of the process were not fully understood for many more decades, fracking was created.

It wasn't until the 1930s that the next step in process came. A non explosive nitroglycerin mixture was tested in hopes of keeping newly created cracks open. In 1947 Floyd Farris attempted a similar technique in the Hugoton gas field in Grant County, Kansas. Farris poured nearly 1,000 gallons of gelled gasoline and sand into a well over 2,000 feet below the surface. It was deemed a relative failure, but the study of the gas and oil relationship would further the progress of fracking's development. By 1949 the Halliburton Oil Well Cementing Company would file for a patent on a more refined technique and open two hydraulic fracking sites in Oklahoma and Texas.

Two years later, not far from Drake's well, Terry Pegula was born.

THE POND, THE LETTER, AND THE DREAM

In 1909 dozens of State College natives gathered at a duck pond only a mile from where Pegula Ice Arena stands today and skated across the ice.

The only proof of that moment, a black and white photo showing the people as nearly indistinguishable dots. Some standing, others sitting on the ice in groups, all in the shadow of a snow covered Mount Nittany. It wasn't hockey but it was one of the first documented moments of State College and Penn State's relationship with the ice.

Two years later on December 7, 1911, the first of many attempts to bring hockey in an official capacity to Penn State began, a letter in the Penn State Collegian with a passionate plea for hockey's inclusion into Penn State's athletic pursuits.

"In regards to the question of a hockey team, Penn State in a few years will undoubtedly take it place among the big universities," the letter read. "The surest way to lead up to that is to compete with them in other branches of sport as well as baseball and football.

There is a much greater chance of defeating them in minor sports than major sports and undoubtedly there are many men here who are good hockey players."

"When you consider the good material here and the value of a game like hockey, it seems a shame that Penn State should be one of the few colleges that do not have hockey teams, and that this is owing merely to lack of initiative."

Only a week later an equally passionate response would find its way to the paper. The argument would ring true nearly 100 years later. Hockey is expensive, and there is no place to play it.

"There are two reasons why the writer believes Penn State is not ready for hockey." It reads. "No adequate place to play the game. Lack of money to finance the sport."

By 1914 and the start of World War I, the notion of Penn State adding another sport was a forgotten notion during the war effort.

However just a month following the war's conclusion, Penn State officially introduced hockey as an activity on campus, what amounted to a gym class was the school's first foray into the sport on any official basis, even if strictly academic. Somewhere in there, the seed was planted.

Even so hockey had a shaky existence for the next several decades on campus bouncing between rinks and degrees of competition and consistency. In the 1930s, the team played on what amounted to frozen tennis courts. In the 1940s frozen fields on the west side of campus hosted the team while briefly at the varsity level but not the Division I level.

By 1955, things began to get more official as an outdoor rink was built in the area of the current Lasch Football Building. By 1960, the building had a roof and Penn State hockey had a home.

If it sounds confusing, that's because it was. Prior to the start of the Division I program Penn State played hockey at varsity, non varsity and club levels. The distinctions are small and the result of college athletics' post-war boom and changing ways. In the broadest sense Penn State hockey existed in very loose terms compared to today's fairly black and white classifications.

In 1971 Penn State hockey started an era of non-varsity hockey that would become the foundation of its modern Division I program. Head coach Larry Hendry was the first, and only for one season. Hendry now works as the head marshall at the 18th tee at Augusta National, making him one of the more interesting ties to Penn State hockey.

In 1978, the most familiar form of Penn State hockey slowly took shape as the ice pavilion was repurposed for an indoor practice facility used for multiple sports including football, and the Icers were once again relegated to the great outdoors for two seasons.

The Greenberg Ice Pavilion not far from the old rink, would become the new face of hockey in Penn State.

The economy struggled and the gas crisis of the 1970s coupled with an uncertain future turned Greenberg from a building planned for just over 4,000 seats to on with just over 1,000. The building was intended to include u-shaped seating configuration but construction crews hit solid rock, so the solution was a rink with seating all on one side.

Penn State's potential Division I plans were set aside yet again for a more conservative option moving forward. It was a tough blow to those dreams, but it was not the first nor the last time hockey would take that hit.

Greenberg opened in 1981 and for the next 30 years it would be the much beloved home of Penn State hockey. In 1984 the team would win its first club national title, but it wasn't until Joe Battista came back to his alma mater in 1987 that things started rolling.

A native of Pittsburgh and a native of hockey, Battista had always been around a rink. In the wake of the 1980 Lake Placid Olympics, Battista was like any kid with dreams of glory.

By the time he made his way to play for Penn State he thought he would be helping the Nittany Lions finally make that Division I leap. Like so many times before, it didn't happen, and Battista played for the Icers at the club level, graduating in 1983. Battista left, working for the Pittsburgh Penguins' marketing department for a few years before moving on to help coach at Culver Military Academy.

The academy was a high level coaching opportunity to work with some of the best and brightest players coming into the sport. All told CMA has produced 22 NHL players with seven currently on rosters, headlined by Minnesota Wild defenseman Ryan Suter.

There wasn't much reason to leave in 1987, but Penn State kept calling Battista and eventually he relented. If the team wasn't Division I by the end of five years, he would move on. Or so he thought.

What unfolded instead was two decades of dominance.

Battista, for all of his energy and enthusiasm doesn't like to take the credit when it comes to Penn State making it to the Division I level. In truth the Pegula gift was the catalyst to that move, however it is impossible to deny the foundation Battista laid to prepare Penn State for that day.

On the ice it took just three years for Battista to win his first national title during the 1989-90 season, his first of six while at Penn State.

The formula itself wasn't overly complicated. Penn State recruited players eyeing the option of Division 3 play. Greenberg was full every single game, students and fans packing the stands. The atmosphere was fantastic, and in many cases the Penn State education carried more weight than competing schools. The choice was supposed to seem obvious, and it was.

The on ice success wasn't hard to explain, but what made the Icers' program stand out was the off-ice infrastructure. Battista created a coalition of people that supported the program as the Icers continued to play as a club team. An academic advisor, programs for games, a CNET television show, the games were even broadcast on the radio. At the end of the day the Icers were run like a Division I program.

The Icers legacy is that foundation, which peaked with national titles five of six years from 1997-2003. The depth of the program was unprecedented and the interwoven stories of players and coaches from Providence to Ohio and beyond still stretches across hockey at all levels.

Penn State has in its own way always had hockey. The Division I program would solidify what had already existed, and what the dream had been for so many years.

Attempts were made. Battista was on the losing end of more than a few intense and well thought-out proposals to bring high level hockey to Penn State. Much like the arguments nearly 100 years before him, the resistance was the same.

There was no place to play the games, and no money to pay for it.

And then the phone rang.

DINNER AND A DONATION

In the winter of 2005, Joe Battista and his family sit down to eat a meal together -- a rarity in a coach's life -- and the phone rings.

Because, of course.

And Battista's wife Heidi answers it, looks at her husband, and hands him the phone. "Make it quick" she says in a way that sounds much more like an order than a request. So Joe takes the phone, unsure of who is on the other end, yet fairly sure it doesn't matter.

As it turned out, it was Terry Pegula. At the time that didn't mean much to Battista, who proceeded to answer a few of Pegula's questions; questions that had been asked and answered a million times before. Why doesn't Penn State play Division I hockey? Why doesn't Penn State play other Big Ten teams?

"Do you know Kelly's Steakhouse?" Pegula asked. "Meet me there in 15 minutes and I'll buy you dinner."

And then he hung up.

Battista looked at his wife, who knew, because she always did, that Joe was about to go. A brief lecture about how often hockey takes precedence over the family later, and he was in fact out the door to meet a man he really didn't know.

But Battista did know Pegula after all. Terry had taken his son to a hockey camp Joe was coaching at, and they had spoken briefly. The unexpected dinner was suddenly not so bizarre, but there was still no indication that it would be so fruitful. Battista ordered steak, as one does, and Terry wasted little time getting down to business. "What would it take" Pegula asked between bites.

For a man who had spent his life explaining why the Icers should be a Division I team and also explaining why they weren't, this was a run -of- the -mill question. Joe spouted off a number that had become his go-to answer.

"Fifty million," Battista replied.

And Terry Pegula leaned back in his chair, raising his hands to rub his neck.

"I think I can help you with that, " he said with a smile.

When Battista got home, he finally found out who he had really been talking to. A simple Google search brought up Pegula's credentials, ones that made him the largest private owner of gas and oil wells east of the Mississippi River. "This one might be for real!!" Battista yelled to Heidi.

And it was.

Although it wasn't so simple.

■ ■ ■

Terrence Pegula was born March 27, 1951 in Carbondale PA, part of the northern and often forgotten reaches of the state. Pegula would eventually make his way to Penn State, earning his degree in petroleum and natural gas engineering. Following his graduation in 1973, Pegula went on to work for Getty Oil in Texas.

In 1983, Pegula was ready to make his own mark on the world, and with the help of a small loan from his family he founded East Resources. By 2000, the company had made its first gas discoveries in central New York state and north-central Pennsylvania, a region increasingly known for its rich Marcellus Shale gas a mile or so beneath the surface. It would make him rich, richer than anyone's wildest dreams. Not so far away from Edwin Drake's Titusville well, where the entire industry first began to boom, it was a fitting, time-is-a-flat-circle way for him to make his fortune. But in 2005, Pegula had yet to reach billionaire status. That would come later.

Like so many times before, Penn State's foray into hockey hit a major financing snag as the stock market contracted in 2007. Penn State was in no position to commit to such an expensive project and neither was Pegula. It was the latest, and perhaps the hardest, blow Battista and the hockey dream took. It was one thing to find that kind of money, and quite another to find it in the worst economy since the Depression. So the dream was tabled, yet again.

Fast-forward five years to May of 2010, with Battista watching TV in bed next to his wife. In 2006 he had left coaching, handing over the reins to his former assistant and Providence hockey native Scott Balboni, a barrel-chested man who had helped reinvigorate Battista's coaching energy midway through his time at Penn State. Battista had shifted back to his marketing roots. Working with the Nittany Lion Club, business was always on his mind.

Flipping through the channels, Battista settled on one of the many business shows, something in the background and not much more. And there it was, a small bit of news crawling inconspicuously across the bottom of the screen, just something amid the noise. Battista could have missed it.

But he didn't.

"Royal Dutch Shell buys East Resources for $4.7 billion"

Battista shook his wife. "Terry sold the company, " he said, mouth agape. "Terry sold the company. He sold the company"

The dream was alive and kicking.

From there things kicked into high gear. Even without the gift officially on the books, Battista began to make trips with Terry and a growing group of people, checking out other venues. Minnesota, Ohio, Boston University, Notre Dame. It was a collection of rinks that would give Penn State an idea of what they were up against. And Pegula was sold.

Just minutes after a tour of the Boston University facilities with coach Mike Eruzione, captain of the US men's hockey team at the 1980 Olympics, Battista got the news. Crossing the busy confusion of a Boston street, his phone buzzed and when he looked down he stopped dead in his tracks.

"Just signed hockey agreement" it read. "It's a great day for hockey in Happy Valley."

It was August 25, 2010. Battista admits he cried, and a friend with him urged him to continue on, but Battista stopped again to re-read the text. Nearly a month later, on September 17, the Pegulas' initial gift of a staggering $88 million was announced to Penn State's Board of Trustees. Penn State was officially, finally, on the path to Division I hockey. On their way to Hockey Valley.

From there a steering committee was created. At first it was a small, self-named Frozen Five, which then quickly expanded to a larger group, a Who's Who of Penn State administrators tackling every conceivable angle. By 2012, at least 11 different people had held a major role of some kind or another in this committee named Project Ice. In the wake of the Sandusky scandal Dave Joyner stepped in for Tim Curley. David Gray, Ford Stryker, Rod Kirsch, Rick Kaluza, Greg Myford, Cliff Benson, Al Horvath, Teresa Davis, Mark Bodenzhatz and Battista himself all filtered into the project to help with their areas of expertise. It truly was all hands on deck.

But the program still needed a coach. On January 15 of 2011, that search was launched. The search itself was fairly straightforward: a checklist of 20 items was created to rank and differentiate the candidates. It included everything from the basics of head coaching experience to a comfort level with modern technology. Penn State wanted the right coach, and that meant a certain need to be picky. The committee talked to national title winners and coaches with current NHL jobs, but it had to be the right hire, not just the right splash.

By the end of the process, 10 candidates had been interviewed by phone and a final three interviewed in person. And one of those final three was Guy Gadowsky, of Princeton University.

Appropriately enough, Guy's interview was the result of not just his own success, but also word of mouth. Everywhere Battista traveled, he heard good things about Gadowsky. Finally, Joe planned a trip to Princeton to see for himself, even if on the record he was checking out the rink to see what Pegula Ice Arena might be like in the future. In reality, it was much less about the ice at Hobey Baker Rink, and much more about the man on it.

Battista came away impressed. Gadowsky's enormous positive energy was infectious and afterwards Battista contacted Terry Pegula, who had stayed hands off the entire time. "I'll see the baby when it's born" he would say, but Battista needed him to meet Guy. Now that Terry and his wife Kim were new owners of the Sabres, it only took a short drive to Buffalo for a game to put Gadowsky, Battista and the Pegulas in the same room.

As the other three talked, Battista waited in the back of the suite. And waited. And waited. At last, he waited no more as Kim walked straight up to Battista and said the words he hoped to hear.

"He's our guy."

So in April of 2011, Guy Gadowsky became the first head coach in the history of Penn State Division I hockey. He would coach the Icers in their final season, a move that would prove to be pivotal in the development of the program as Gadowsky and his staff began to implement their system a season earlier than the leap into Division I play.

Things were not entirely smooth sailing from that point on. The $88 million left an uncomfortable gap in Penn State's projected costs to construct the arena, finance the scholarships, and a myriad of peripheral costs. Being close to the necessary financial goal was helpful, but would have created a whole new set of obstacles. With no good way to raise the extra funds, there was even a short conversation regarding whether the gift should be turned down entirely.

It wasn't. Because in 2012, the Pegulas stood in that gap themselves after a few passionate sale pitches from Penn State. Fourteen million dollars later the program was funded, complete with an endowment fund of $10 million to make it self-sufficient. In total, the Pegulas would gift $102 million in pursuit of the best facility and program in Division I hockey.

"A program is only as strong as the student-athletes who choose to dedicate their time and talent to making it great," said Pegula. "We hope that through these scholarships, Penn State will be able to build a team of rising hockey stars who will succeed athletically and academically at the University. We also want to make sure that these young people have a facility which will allow them to fulfill their potential and be the best possible representatives of the University and Penn State Intercollegiate Athletics. "

Pegula wanted a building that would last a lifetime, the fastest ice in North America, and a state-of-the-art ice system. So there would be battles, because coveted ribbon banners over there meant fewer longed-for perks somewhere else. A give and take, and a win and a loss.

Seven years after that steak dinner, and 100 years after that letter to The Collegian, Penn State hockey was a Division I program. The puck was dropped for the first time, and in that moment, Hockey Valley was truly born.

LIFE AT 40,000 FEET

Fifty thousand miles could fly you across the country 24 times if you were to take the shortest route. That's 12 round trips from New York to LA. A prodigious span of travel above everything the nation has to offer, from the purple mountains majesties to those amber waves of grain, you'd see it all from above.

Penn State assistant coaches Matt Lindsay and Keith Fisher have put in more than their fair share of those air miles. In fact, Fisher guesses that 50,000 miles through the air and on the ground encompasses just his past 12 months of travel alone. By his estimation that number is actually lower than in the past since things have gotten slightly easier as the years fly by. The two of them cover more ground than maybe any other staff on campus. Where some staffs may focus on a few states, Lindsay and Fisher focus on an entire continent.

Hockey clinics help, bringing players from all over to the same place, and the Internet has done wonders for turning over rocks from miles away. At the end of the day, though, there is no way around the travel. If a player calls Fairbanks, Alaska home, there is only one good way to connect with that family. If another spends his time in Buffalo, you make the drive.

The endless recruiting territory is a stark contrast to Penn State football's luxuries. The program has split Pennsylvania into small sections, and each of the half dozen or so assistant coaches get a small slice of the pie. Meanwhile it's commercial flights and long nights to some of the farthest and coldest reaches of the continent for Fisher and Lindsay. This is what they've been doing for much of their lives, and a place they've worked much of their careers to get to.

Inside Pegula Ice Arena their offices are just feet apart, across the hallway from Gadowsky and Director of Operations Alex Dawes. TVs are mounted to the walls, posters from various Penn State seasons accumulating next to them. It's the best way to remember all the history packed into the past few years.

The catch for these two is the difference in personalities. Fisher looks the part of a head coach and doesn't pretend that isn't a career goal. He's stern and calculated, he commands attention and he gets it. Lindsay is no less serious about his job, but his big smile and warm personality projects a certain sense of being thrilled by each and every current day. Their relationship itself does not clash, but it's impossible to ignore the almost comical differences in personality. The reason it works is a shared interest in Penn State's success, and shared experiences on the roads that led them to Penn State in the first place.

Lindsay's journey started in Massachusetts, where his coaching career began after graduating from Williams College. Then it was Utica, and then Hobart, both jobs as assistant coaches. From there, Lindsay made his way to Colorado College and then landed his first Division I job at Robert Morris as the team's video coordinator and recruiting assistant. It was early in RMU's Division

I existence, so resources and pay were limited, but Lindsay was finally in Division I.

Then one day he saw a listing. Princeton hockey was hiring its staff under soon-to-be head coach Guy Gadowsky. And so Lindsay applied, not knowing if he would get the call, but hoping, fingers crossed. Lindsay had a background lining up with Gadowsky's both alum of Colorado College and Gadowsky a native of Alberta, a place Lindsay was familiar with from recruiting. It was a perfect resume boost at the perfect moment.

In Minnesota, Fisher was headed on a path would also lead to Princeton. Growing up in Minnesota, hockey was a part of life. In many ways Minnesota is a mixture of American and Canadian cultures, hockey bleeding down across the border to a state with a rich hockey history.

It was only natural when Fisher found himself working as an undergrad assistant at St. Cloud State with a program that would become of the nation's most consistent farther down the road.

From there, it was the Omaha Lancers of the USHL, another step towards bigger and better things. While in Omaha, Fisher helped coach and recruit NHL first-round draft picks Keith Ballard and Nick Petrecki, and 11 NHL players, including Matt Carle and Paul Stastny. It all culminated with a Clark Cup championship in 2001 and two more regular-season titles in 2002 and 2005.

Then one day, like Lindsay, he saw Princeton's listing. Although Fisher had met Gadowsky at a rink in Buffalo of all places, he was no more a friend than Lindsay, crossing his fingers not far away. The rest is Princeton history.

Over the next six seasons, Lindsay and Fisher would work together on the recruiting trail and on the bench. What would become Penn State's coaching staff one day first put together a

Princeton team that made the postseason in 2008 and 2009, including a school-record 22 wins in 2009. And then the call came.

"I knew that Guy was up talking to Penn State," Lindsay recalled. "And he called me after midnight on his drive back and said, 'How would you like to come with me to Penn State?' I said 'Yes, of course. And probably would have called him the next day if he hadn't.'"

There were challenges ahead for both assistants. They were primary points of contact for the program on the road and its creation came as the crisis of the Sandusky scandal unfolded. It became an unavoidable topic with recruits and the college hockey world, watching the birth of Penn State's fledgling program. Recruiting to an unproven program would have been hard enough, but the uncertainties of what lay ahead for Penn State athletics did little to help the cause.

"We would have people ask us if the Pegulas were going to take back the gift," Fisher noted.

"We would hear from people that would say the building wasn't going to be built anymore, or that there wasn't going to be a program."

Fortunately those worries were short lived, and did little to change the general concept of what an early Penn State player might look like. Fisher and Lindsay knew that the biggest names in the sport weren't going to fall out of the sky. The men that would be the foundation for Penn State hockey would have to be a different breed of player. So they targeted captains. Late bloomers. Players with something to prove.

And it worked. Penn State's first few rosters were littered with captains from their previous teams and players who came into their own, blooming into Big Ten award level contenders.

Once they got on campus Fisher, Lindsay and Gadowsky did what they do best, developed talent, and the results, even in defeat, often spoke for themselves.

"I don't know if I want give away our secrets," Fisher said of the program's ability to develop players. "But we feel good about how we do it." One NHL GM remarked that Princeton was a great hidden gem in hockey development. The same could be said of Penn State's results now, the likes of Kevin Kerr and Denis Smirnov blooming far earlier than even the staff expected.

As a result, the travel has diminished slightly. Recruiting is no less a grind, but far less difficult a sell. Players and advisors reach out to Penn State, making introductions instead of Fisher and Lindsay. And after the season the Nittany Lions had in 2016-17, that will not be slowing down.

"We wouldn't have gotten this far without that season at the club level and the success we had that first season at Division I," Fisher added, proof of concept confirmed as Penn State held its own night after night. How long the staff remains together will be an interesting dynamic to watch. Fisher was a finalist for the Princeton job two years ago before staying at Penn State.

Lindsay no less the rising commodity himself.

Whatever the future holds for these two, Penn State's success be attributed to many things, not the least of all, long flights and even longer drives. It is a program that found its footing one recruit and 50,000 miles at a time.

BETTER LIVING THROUGH COACHING

It sounded like a gunshot as the butt end of a stick slammed past the face of an unsuspecting Edmonton Oiler. For those behind the corner glass at Northland Coliseum in the late 1970s, it was something so loud and unexpected that they sat in stunned silence.

If the act was unintentional, the slow lowering of the stick from the glass did little to support that theory; a message had been sent. This was no mistake.

A few rows up from the ice, a young Guy Gadowsky tried to catch a glimpse of the perpetrator in front of him. And he did, a brief sighting through the crowd of the one and only Mr. Hockey himself, Gordie Howe, who smiled as his stick returned to the ice and he skated back to the bench.

And Gadowsky soaked it all in, a moment that to this day he remembers fondly.

Well before Gadowsky began his hockey baptism, explorer Anthony Henday and the Hudson's Bay Company would see to the building of Fort Edmonton along the banks of the North

Saskatchewan River. The fort would act not only as an outpost, but a trading center for the company's furs and other goods.

While the indigenous population had called that area home for years, 1795 would mark the first established European settlement in what would one day become the city of Edmonton. By 1892, the population had grown to 700 residents, and just 13 years later would become the capital city of Alberta as the territory joined the confederation.

Fittingly, Edmonton's founding enterprise has grown much like the city itself. While Edmonton sits as the most northern major city in North America, the Hudson's Bay Company now operates retail stores in multiple countries and has grown into a multi-billion dollar business. As for Henday, his name is atop Highway 216 which encircles the city for more than 70 miles, a bypass for trucks and travelers alike.

Known affectionately as the Gateway to The North, Edmonton has never really shaken off its status as the last stop before the wild. Just over 1,400 miles from the north pole, little lies beyond the reaches of the city limits aside from sand oil refineries and the vast wilderness of Canada's northern fringes.

There is only so much frontier that you can erase. Edmonton is still an outpost, but far from a lonely one. As Gadowsky grew up, that frontier became his backyard. At a young age he found himself waiting just inside the door for his mother to tie his skates. There was no reason to do it at the pond since the roads were frozen, sometimes in perpetuity.

In an age where mothers let their sons wander without much concern, Gadowsky would skate down the street, stick in hand and learn the game every Canadian is taught to play.

Competition was natural in his household. His older sisters swam, and his father was a gym teacher. Many years later, Gadowsky still remembers his first hockey game at the age of five or six, a stinging lament that his team lost, an equally boyish disappointment that the winning goal was scored by a *girl*. And yes, he remembers her name.

'Cathy Dixson."

The Edmonton Oilers joined the NHL in 1979 when Gadowsky was 11. Edmonton was already a great sports town with a major league soccer team, a Triple-A baseball team and a Canadian football team. What more, one thinks, could a boy ask for?

Gadowsky was there the first night the Montreal Canadians came to Edmonton, the fans packing into seats around the ice to catch a glimpse of a premier Canadian hockey franchise. Edmonton's eventual rise to the top of hockey was not far behind, but in those early stages, it was like looking at the hockey gods themselves.

Back home, the aspirations were slightly more realistic. Gadowsky watched as Gord Whittaker made his way out of the neighborhood and on to Colorado College and was later drafted by the Winnipeg Jets in 1984. Whittaker would end up playing in the Jets' system and overseas, but the path and the career weren't the important part. Whittaker was the oldest kid on the block living the dream. In the way of boys everywhere, everything Whittaker touched was thought of as gold, so if Colorado College was good enough for him, it was good enough for Gadowsky.

It made the offer irresistible when Colorado College offered Gadowsky a place on its team. In retrospect, Gadowsky may have been better off with a additional year in juniors.

He was smaller than his teammates and not as strong. An extra year would have prepared him for his career at the college level.

But even in a household with plenty of athletes, academics were still a priority. By the time the nest had been emptied, Gadowsky's mother would go on to become a librarian while his father continued to teach. His college offer may have come a year too soon, for hockey, but Gadowsky was ready for the rest of his life to start.

By the time Gadowsky finished his fourth year at Colorado College he had learned more than a few lessons he would take with him into coaching, but not before doing whatever he could to find a home playing the game.

And that meant everywhere and anywhere. Gadowsky played roller hockey first, then for three more ice hockey teams including a stint overseas as he tried to move up the endlessly changing hockey scene. In Sweden, he honed stick skills. In North America playing the AHL for the St. John's Maple Leafs he worked some of the more traditional hockey skill sets. It was a constant learning experience over many years.

The entire travel saga would culminate in Gadowsky's selection to the Canadian National Team in 1993, which at the time did not include NHL players. It was a unique honor for the Edmonton native but one that would prove to be a key moment in Gadowsky's career.

Gadowsky made a handful of appearances on the active roster during his year on the national team, but was eventually cut.

It was a blow to be sure, but he wasn't going to go out that easily. A season in Germany taught Gadowsky a European mindset focused on skills and stickwork. Then it was to Prince Edward Island back in the AHL for a season in the Ottawa Senators' organization, and then to Fresno. In 1995-96 he earned league MVP and first-team all-star recognition while in Fresno having totaled 59 goals and 29 assists that year. His best for last.

Around, up and and down, all across the hockey ladder just looking for a home.

Gadowsky would find that home in coaching.

The timeline is messy, another series of quick moves, but each with meaningful moments. Gadowsky coached in Fresno and then San Jose where he met his wife before making his way back to Fresno yet again. His first year coaching in Fresno as part of the West Coast Hockey League he led the team to the playoffs and 38-wins earning WCHL Coach of the Year honors. By the time he left he had become the winningest coach in the franchise's history.

Coaching was natural for Gadowsky, but he quickly discovered he had plenty more to learn.

And so as he applied for the head coaching job at Alaska-Fairbanks heading into the 1999 season, his life was about to begin a new chapter, much as the century itself was set to change.

■ ■ ■

In September of 2011, a Google Street View car rode through the beautiful desolation of Alaska's Route 11. It is a road in the most basic sense of the definition, just holding together as it winds through the mountains and tundra, the only sign that humanity exists.

The road is there almost out of obligation, a desire to prove that man could not leave so much land unconquered.

Functionally, it connects the rest of Alaska to an outcropping of Halliburton buildings near Prudhoe Bay, just a short distance from the Beaufort Sea on the state's most northern banks. If not for those buildings, and if not for that road, the world may have very well ended somewhere in the permafrost and ever confused daylight.

The edge of the world, if it is anywhere, might just be north of Fairbanks. To the east the Yukon lies not far away, and with it land nearly untouched save a handful of airstrips.

The only respite is the six hour drive south to Anchorage that takes you past Denali, a mountain so large that it can create its own weather systems. At just over 20,300 feet it is the third tallest peak in the world, towering over neighboring mountains.

It comes as no surprise that nearly all 32,000 Fairbanks residents cling to their hockey team; a bubble in the middle of the frontier coming together as a community. The Carlson Center, opened in 1990 holding 4,595 fans who show up in spades every week to root on the Nanooks. It's even less of a surprise that as Gadowsky joined that tight-knit community it would be the catalyst that would change his life.

For the first two seasons the team struggled, winning just six and eight games respectively. But then the tide began to turn. Fairbanks started the 2001-02 season strong and over the course of the year would beat Michigan in Ann Arbor; Ohio State and Notre Dame en route to a 22-12-3 finish and fourth place in the CCHA.

With that success, Gadowsky got his first lessons in the power of outside noises. Trips to the gas station and fans would know the score; the grocery store, the same story.

Everywhere, a city in the middle of nowhere was coming together around their team.

Gadowsky would later compare it to the pressures and sense of ownership felt at Penn State, albeit smaller in size, but no less passionate.

While the team never made the NCAA Tournament under Gadowsky, that eventual appearance in 2008 was the byproduct of the foundation he helped lay. For all good coaches, bigger and better things come calling. When Princeton made that call in 2004, Gadowsky took it. The job brought him back to the states and closer to his wife's eastern ties.

There was a challenge unique to the Princeton job. Gadowsky was not an Ivy League product. It was a point of quiet criticism of the hire and an equally quiet point of motivation for Gadowsky to prove that he belonged. The raised eyebrows were only accentuated by the fact Gadowsky's name never surfaced in the media during Princeton's coaching search. Gadowsky seemed to appear out of nowhere to take the job. And considering he was making the trip from Fairbanks back into civilization at large, that wasn't entirely untrue.

The good news was steady progress. In the first four years of Gadowsky's tenure, he guided the Tigers to gradual and increasing success. In 2007, the Tigers made the NCAA Tournament after winning only eight games just a few years prior.

But the postseason challenge of facing North Dakota was no small task. A 5-1 loss to an eventual semifinalist was a lesson of how far Princeton had to go as a program, as a coaching staff, and as players.

So in 2008, it was back to square one, and the Tigers improved yet again, picking up 22 wins and heading back to the NCAA Tournament. Gadowsky proved he belonged, and onlookers noticed. More than a few NHL scouts called Princeton one of the great development secrets in the game. In the first round of the NCAA Tournament it looked as though those postseason lessons had been learned. The Tigers led by two goals against Minnesota-Duluth with 39 seconds to go.

And then Duluth scored.

And then with 0.8 seconds left, they scored again.

Princeton lost in overtime, something of a foregone conclusion by the time the clock finished out that final fraction of a second. Just like that a shot at the Frozen Four had turned into a flight back home.

Gadowsky doesn't remember much about the weeks that followed, only a blur of shock and recovery. As for the program, all great climbs involve an inevitable downturn in a world of ever-changing rosters. Seasons of 12 and 17 wins saw the program headed back towards postseason play.

But then Joe Battista walked through the door of Hobey Baker Memorial Rink.

ONE LAST HURRAH

2012-13

Yellow.

That's the color anyone who spent time in the Greenberg Ice Pavilion should remember.

That yellow haze splashed across everything. It challenged white balances to make photos look as if they were indeed shot in this century. It challenged video producers to make local news broadcasts seem capable of quality control.

The culprit was a vintage florescent lighting system that was probably invented in the era of mercury in high school science classrooms. Whatever forgotten science created it had been abandoned, but Greenberg, continued the tradition along with cement stands and no-frills entertainment beyond the game.

None of that mattered the first time Penn State hockey skated as a Division I program in 2012. The air could have been purple or orange or blue. The game could have been played in the dark.

Smiles.

That's the other thing splashed across the building. Penn State could have lost that game by 100 goals and it wouldn't have mattered. The Nittany Lions were a Division I program. A dream finally realized, huge renderings of Pegula Ice Arena behind the benches, drenched in yellow light.

When the puck finally dropped, the crowd of 1,300 was packed to the rafters. It was just a small percentage of Pegula's capacity, but they didn't need very long to be reminded that game was taking place. Penn State didn't score first, because 2:43 into the game American International hit the back of the net, beating Matt Skoff in his first start for the blue and white. He would soon be a staple in goal for the Nittany Lions. But the smiles stayed.

And they got wider, as almost exactly two minutes later forward Casey Bailey scooped up a rebound and flicked it into the net to tie the game, sending the crowd into a frenzy.

A goal, it happened. It was real. The dream was real. It was here, at last.

Of course not all dreams end like you wish, the back-and-forth action would hit its peak as Taylor Holstrom tied the game with just over six minutes to go. Eventually the horn would sound and with it regulation ended. The night was just a Penn State goal away from perfection. Yet it was Jon Puskar winning it for AIC in the final minute of overtime.

But the smiles stayed.

Joe Battista slapped his hands together in the back of the media area, a precariously placed overhang above the net, just below an ever-excited air compressor that would often knock a light or two out of commission. He was frustrated, a team so close to the perfect opening night. But mostly he was happy. It was finally happening.

Those smiles made their way to the bench too. After the game Guy Gadowsky was smiling ear to ear, his teeth clenched in an odd way as if he was holding back from shouting out his love for the game.

Of course Greenberg was happening too, a building that nearly breathed in its own right.

The first press conference after the first game was highlighted not by quotes but the Zamboni garage door opening, the air compressors with unspecified purposes going off.

"I am thrilled right now," Gadowsky said sitting at a folding table, shouting ever so slightly as Greenberg clanged and banged. "I thought we played great. We had no idea what we had. We had no idea if we would be ill-matched. We generated a lot of offense.

Twenty shots each period is fantastic. I love the student section and to see the crowd, it was fantastic. This is why recruits and other people come here."

It was, to say the least, noisy.

But the smiles stayed.

The following night Penn State got a chance to win, and did just that. In an attempt to get early state-wide interest in the program, the Nittany Lions played AIC in Wilkes-Barre in front of a much more Pegula-sized crowd of nearly 5,400. The Nittany Lions won 4-3.

David Glen scored in the first period and then again just 38 seconds into overtime to secure the first win in Penn State hockey's Division I history.

A week later against Buffalo State, fans would get a glimpse of the kind of offense-minded program Penn State would become years later. In the first period the Nittany Lions blasted 19 shots on net while Skoff had to stop just six shots all period.

In spite of the foreshadowing, Penn State lost, a great night of offense met by an even better night of goaltending. Buffalo State skated away with a single game series, 3-0 victory.

The effort would continue though, and the goals followed along Penn State would bounce back the next day against RIT, firing 42 shots on goal while California native and part-time surfer PJ Musico stopped 22 shots. The Nittany Lions squeaked out the victory to the tune of a 3-2 game.

"Absolutely I'm happy," Gadowsky would say of the team's now 2-2 start. "It was tremendous for us to win at RIT in front of a great environment. You don't know until the future, but I think that winning at RIT was a tremendous win for us as a program and our confidence. We aren't changing our goals in terms of the season. It has never been about wins or losses, just making progress forward. If we played really, really well and still didn't win, we'll be happy with the progress. Now that we've won a couple big games, our focus isn't just going to change. It's going to be about building a foundation all year long, and if we do a good job wins will be a byproduct of that. But we aren't changing our focus. No way."

A week later, the back-to-back nights against different opponents continued, and so too did the goals and the offense. Penn State's shot count continued to rise, as the Nittany Lions beat Army 5-0, and then the following night crushed Sacred Heart 6-3, allowing just 19 shots on goal.

The culmination of the early success came as Penn State faced Buffalo State yet again, this time back in Greenberg. The Nittany Lions had fallen short just a few weeks prior, but showcased their new found confidence to a sold out crowd, eager to see what the road had taught their new team.

By the end of the night Penn State had won 4-2, three straight goals turning a 1-0 deficit into a 3-1 margin: David Glen scoring unassisted with just over three minutes to play to seal the deal at 4-2. In the process Penn State outshot Buffalo State by 24, a dominating performance on the offensive end of the ice.

Of course there was always bound to be a bump in the road. Even though the schedule mixed club and lower DI teams against Penn State, these were teams that knew their own identity and were far more familiar with life at the Division I level than Penn State.

Predictably, the early excitement started to wear off as those realities settled in. Penn State would split a series against Air Force, both teams winning 5-1. David Glen hit the six goal mark, and the Nittany Lions scored twice in an empty net to finish their win.

At the time Penn State didn't know it, but 4-1 and 2-0 losses to No. 8 Union would serve as a marker for the Nittany Lions' growth as a program. Union would travel to Pegula Ice Arena years later, and Penn State would face the program yet again during its first-ever NCAA Tournament appearance.

The 2012 Union losses began what many expected all along despite the smiles. The Nittany Lions were playing moderately well, trying hard, improving in areas that they needed to improve, but the team was losing. This wasn't a surprise, least of all to the many observers who assumed Penn State's first few years of Division I existence would be primarily defeats.

And that wouldn't turn out to be entirely untrue. Penn State won just once in a span of seven games and for the most part those games were one-sided on the score sheet. An overtime 5-4 loss to Holy Cross followed by a 4-1 loss to the Crusaders was a reminder of how small the margin of error can be at the highest levels. The Nittany Lions beat Fredonia 4-0, the only respite in a sea of challenges.

It was an important teaching moment for Penn State, and there was a small bit of solace to be found. The Nittany Lions were losing, but they looked like they belonged. In turn it was not hard to imagine the program learning how to win in the process. Winning can mask a team's issues in many ways. Losing brings those issues to the forefront, and in turn makes them easier to identify and improve.

One such issue was finding ways to finish chances against better opponents. Penn State faced Robert Morris, a team not shy about its enthusiasm for knocking the Nittany Lions down a few pegs. Penn State pounded away at the net: 12 shots in the first, 13 in the second and 15 in the third. By the end of the game, the shot count was a lopsided 40-29 in Penn State's favor, but Robert Morris won the game itself 3-2. Penn State failed to score at all after two quick goals in the opening 3:25 of the second period.

"I felt like we deserved the result tonight," Gadowsky said. "I was happy with a lot of things that we did. Robert Morris is a good team. They just took three of four points from Ohio State last weekend."

This would be the challenge for years to come. Penn State could get shots on net, but the quality chances and goals from those chances were far fewer. It was a fun style of play, but it required that players crash the net, pounce on loose pucks and create chaos in front.

It wasn't always pretty, but without the pure skill players in Penn State's future, it was the best equation for winning.

It gave Penn State players a bit of hope to hang on to each night. When the offense worked, it steamrolled across defenses. Two or three minute bursts blew games wide open or suddenly closed a gap. Years later at Pegula, those kinds of bursts would be the sort of thing to wake up the crowd, giving the Nittany Lions one of the best home ice advantages in the sport. As it did in Greenberg, the attentive crowd would often make all the difference.

Following the Robert Morris loss, Penn State was banking on that crowd again, this time in Pittsburgh for the Three Rivers Classic. The Nittany Lions may have been the fan favorite, but lost to Robert Morris again in a lopsided 6-0 rout. Even in its early years, Penn State was a team known for not rolling over. And so the Nittany Lions would hit the ice yet again the following night.

In front of over 10,000 fans at Consol Energy Center the loss was firmly in the rearview as Penn State prepared to face future Big Ten foe Ohio State. For a heavily partisan Nittany Lion crowd, playing the Buckeyes, let alone with a brand new hockey team, was enough to energize everyone in the building.

Penn State found a way to survive as Ohio State opened the scoring 3:56 into the game.

Curtis Loik tied the game for the Nittany Lions before Holstrom and Bailey both scored in just over two minutes late in the first period to push Penn State ahead 3-1.

Of course Ohio State, a team used to the adversity of Division I hockey, wasn't about to give up. With future Ottawa Senator Ryan Dzingel at forward, it didn't take much to get back into the game. In fact, it took just 2:39 into the second period before Dzingel scored on a breakaway. But Penn State wasn't giving up either and Casey Bailey found the back of the net with nine seconds to play making it 4-2.

Twenty-one seconds into the third period Holstrom scored again, taking a pass from Bailey to push Penn State ahead 5-2. The Bailey-Holstrom connection was only in its infancy, but the two would become cornerstones of Penn State's offense for years, a dynamic duo with powerful shooting from Bailey and one of Penn State's first really great stick players in Holstrom.

That didn't matter much to Dzingel, who scored his second of the night 7:49 into the third period, as Matthew Skoff scrambled in goal to stop 24 shots in the final two periods of play and 36 total for the night.

Ohio State got one final goal with a few minutes to play, and an extra attacker on the ice, but the Buckeyes couldn't equalize, and Penn State skated off by the skin of its teeth with a 5-4 victory. It was a historic win and, the first against a Big Ten team. It wouldn't be the last.

The positive vibes didn't last for long, though. Penn State lost to Connecticut on the road, and to Neumann in overtime back at Greenberg, although Glen and Bailey both hit the double digit mark with 10 goals. Needing momentum to end the season, the Nittany Lions looked to a single game against Vermont in Philadelphia. A crowd of nearly 20,000 packed the Wells Fargo Center, and almost all of them were rooting for Penn State.

"That was a wow moment," Gadowsky would later remark.

For Gadowsky, his team and staff, it was a wow moment, indeed. Penn State had been embraced in Pittsburgh, but for better or worse the 'Burgh has a lukewarm feeling about Penn State's existence. Back home, Greenberg's modest capacity made for a good close-quarters atmosphere, but not too much more.

But a packed NHL building with fans to see Penn State play? That was the first real look at how big the entire undertaking of building a program was. It also demonstrated how much support existed and how high expectations would soon become.

Despite the win, internally the feeling was that Penn State didn't play particularly great that night, but a Holstrom goal 3:11 into regulation and Glen's 11th tally of the year would put the Nittany Lions up 2-0 after the first period. From there it was largely elementary. The crowd roared with every hit, and by the midway point of the second period it was 3-1, the game's final score coming with just 11 seconds to play to make it 4-1.

While Penn State and Gadowsky felt the team could have played better despite the end result, the win was far from unappreciated. For newly-minted Penn State fans, it was a reminder that not all of the sport's biggest names would be the familiar faces of big football brands, and it was a win against a rising power in college hockey.

That wouldn't be the case the following week as Penn State traveled to East Lansing to face Michigan State. The first night's 5-3 loss wasn't without its positives. Penn State managed a three goal second period jumpstarted by Tommy Olczyk's shorthanded score and followed up on with goals from Holstrom and Glen. The negatives were two goals by Michigan State in the same period, two more in the third, and an empty net tally giving for a 5-3 loss.

Yet a second Big Ten win did not seem like an impossible dream.

Of course, that dream wasn't realized easily. Michigan State scored twice in the first period, and nearly held Penn State scoreless in the second period as well before Mark Yanis, a constant physical force on the boards, scored with 32 seconds to go in the period.

While Bailey scored his 12th of the year to tie the game, it was the likes of Max Gardiner, a Minnesota transfer and St Louis Blues draft choice, who had made Bailey's job so easy.

Gardiner, his brother already in the NHL, supplied three assists to reach 16 on the season.

And it was Gardiner who found Bailey, who then found Holstrom for the game winner with just under four minutes to play. In spite of Jake Hildebrand making a whopping 47 saves for the Spartans, Penn State made the most of its chances. They had learned that lesson along the way, and sealed the deal. Skoff had continued to improve and was the proverbial reliable netminder. His 10 third period saves and 31 overall were no small part of the 3-2 victory.

In the final home series of the year, Penn State dispatched Alabama-Huntsville in a club-era throwback with 4-0 and 4-3 victories. In a year where nobody knew if Penn State would even win, the Nittany Lions were suddenly 12-13-0, nearly a .500 team.

Visiting Wisconsin, ranked 18th, couldn't have come at a better time for Penn State, but the Badgers won 5-0 despite PJ Musico making 46 saves for Penn State. It was easy to assume Wisconsin would win the following night as well. That may have been what the Badgers were assuming. But if Penn State had learned anything this season, it was a healthy disinterest in giving up. Saturday was Exhibit A in just that. By the night's end Skoff would manage 42 saves but not before Mark Zengerle finally beat him with 3:20 to go in the second period.

Still, it was just 1-0.

Joseph LaBate put Wisconsin up 2-0 in the third period.

But then seven seconds later, Holstrom scored his eighth of the year, the ever present Gardiner with his 18th assist. Six minutes later, Bailey scored on the power play, and all of sudden it was 2-2 late in the third period.

And then, overtime.

If you were writing a movie about this season Penn State would obviously win in overtime. The season had been full of ups and downs, big wins and tough losses. In their first year in Division I, the team had given fans a reason to hope and a reason to be patient. A win against Wisconsin was the perfect way to tie a bow on a little bit of history.

It took a nail-biting four minutes and 26 seconds of a five-minute overtime period, but Penn State finally found that bow.

Taylor Holstrom jumped on a rebound and beat Landon Peterson with Penn State's 36th shot on goal. Penn State's bench cleared, the team swarmed the ice. Everyone believed.

As the teams left the ice there was still a collective wariness of the unknown. This first season had proven Penn State could compete, but the Nittany Lions were set to face Big Ten opponents a year earlier than expected as the Big Ten opted to change its plans. A new home at Pegula would bring new challenges and new expectations. The comforts of Greenberg were no more: the short glass, the smaller crowds, the yellow lights, all things of the past.

"No one knew if we'd even get a Division I win. That wasn't a given," Gadowsky said.

"The first one was a lot of fun. To beat a Big Ten opponent was something that nobody gave us a shot at, and then to go on the road in a Big Ten environment and win, to come away with not one win but two, those were certainly benchmarks that I didn't expect."

"I think we're getting there," he added. "I think the results that we had this year would speak more to that than I expected. As things laid out, we were supposed to have another year before the Big Ten conference formed, but it all got bumped up and we were nervous that we were getting into this too quickly. But you see the wins that we've had and the games that we've played, and you get a lot of confidence from that. We're more prepared now than we were at the start."

And as the lights at Pegula turned on for the first time, they were brighter and hotter than anyone could have ever imagined.

HOME IS WHERE THE HEART IS

Eddie Olczyk had to take a call. He answered the phone as he left the room, walking down a hallway before eventually hanging up and returning the way he came.

"Where are we headed?" his wife Diana asked, knowing all too well what just happened.

"Winnipeg."

The NHL transactions report for November 10th, 1990, would read that Eddie Olczyk had been traded, taking his talents from Toronto to Winnipeg. And so the family packed and prepared for the move 2,000 miles away.

But November 10th would also mark a far more important date in the lives of the Olczyk family. Because the call came as the Olczyks waited in a hospital, and Eddie was taking the call as he walked down a hall past doctors in Diana's labor and delivery suite. It was a day the family would never forget, but for all the right reasons. It was the day their son Tommy was born.

In many respects, that moment set the tone for the early life of one Tommy Olczyk, destined to one day become Penn State hockey's first-ever captain at the Division I level.

Tommy was the first to wear the C in a program unsure of its own future beyond whatever the next game might be.

But before Olczyk ever made it to Penn State, he traveled nearly everywhere else. The first 10 years of his life had moments sown all across the country, an upbringing on the road. His father would play in Winnipeg, then New York, then back to Winnipeg before stints in LA, Pittsburgh and Chicago. The stay in LA lasted only a single season before the elder Olczyk uprooted the family and headed to Pittsburgh over 2000 miles away.

That wasn't easy. Making friends and then losing them, finding a new home and then leaving it; maybe just wise beyond his years or simply just a product of the only life he has known, Olczyk took it in stride, as well as anyone could.

It may have been in his DNA. His older brother played hockey, his uncle is the assistant general manager for the Carolina Hurricanes. Sport and the life that comes with it had been a part of the family for far longer than Tommy.

But it was his mother who got the skates on his feet, one of the first memories Tommy has of hitting the ice. His dad was on the road in some non-specific city, leaving the two of them to their own devices that day. "I remember hitting the boards and falling over,"

Olczyk recalled. "I didn't like it it, and my mom told me to get up and go back out there. And I'm glad she did."

It didn't take long for the sport to find its place in Olczyk's heart and even less time for him to get a grasp of the required skill set. Soon enough he was just like so many other members of his family who had hit the frozen surface before him, eyeing a future in the sport. By 2000, 10 straight years of travel had settled, or at least it appeared to. The Olczyks were in Chicago, the final stop of Eddie's playing career tour. Nearly 20 years in the league, it ended where it all began in 1984. Except the moving wasn't really over, not yet.

Eddie took the job as the Pittsburgh Penguins' head coach, and so the family moved again in 2003. And then again in 2004. "We moved back to Chicago," Olczyk would so eloquently say. "After my dad got canned." It was a short stint in Pittsburgh, a season and a half in the pre-Crosby era. A difficult time for the franchise still finding itself in the final years of Mario Lemieux's time on the ice.

Finally though, life had become Olczyk's own, and with no moving in sight for years more to come. It was a liberating moment, settling down again in Chicago. The next move would be on his own terms and for himself.

In 2007, he headed to Iowa to play for the Sioux City Musketeers in the USHL. His brother Eddie was already there, a small comfort away from home, even as Tommy and his teammates moved into the homes of host families. Time to grow up, and grow up quickly. Of course the challenge in the earliest years of Tommy's career was that name.

Olczyk. It carried a certain weight in hockey circles, and with it a certain skepticism that Tommy had earned a path to bigger and better things in the world of hockey.

It didn't last for long. A likeable personality coupled with the presence of his brother meant the sideways looks and occasional doubting teammates were limited. By his second season in Sioux City, he was just another one of the guys. His third season in 2009 was highlighted by earning the captaincy. And a year later, he earned a call from soon-to-be Penn State coach Guy Gadowsky.

"He called me from the coaches' convention in Florida," Olczyk remembers. "Asked me if I wanted to visit Penn State." It was a big moment in Olczyk's career. Teams had waffled on him, but none had yet offered a trip to campus. When he got to Penn State the offer came shortly thereafter, and there wasn't much doubt at that point where he was headed.

The challenge? Penn State wouldn't be a Division I program for another year after Olczyk enrolled, so he and a handful of other Division I bound players played on Penn State's ACHA team for its final season in Greenberg Ice Pavilion in 2011-12.

That presented its own small frictions There was a certain level of animosity towards the players set to join the Division I team the following year. The Icers had a long and rich history of winning, a big fan base, and were about to write their final chapter, using players with a bit more skill and a bit brighter future in hockey. The walls went up.

But hockey has a funny way of bringing people together, and it didn't take long for those walls to come down. The team would finish just shy of a national title, but far closer than it seemed possible in the early days of the new faces joining an old program. "We wanted to win it for those seniors," Olczyk recalled. "I hate to say regrets in life, but I wish we could go back and win that title."

With a club season done it was time for the bigger show to begin. The first-ever NCAA team approached its first season of ups and downs. The show moved on to even bigger things with the first season at Pegula Ice Arena. Crowds would pack the stands and the stakes became even higher in the Big Ten. Olczyk took on the challenge of being Penn State's captain during a season even more historic than the year before.

That challenge weighed on Olczyk. He was and is by his own admission not the kind of player who would dazzle opponents and fans with his skills. He was the epitome of the kind of player who does all of the little things: the stick checks, the battles in the boards, the hard work in practice. That pressure to produce was heavy and hard to remove. His second season at the Division I level ended with just five goals and five assists.

Penn State entered its second season at Pegula with a new captain, Patrick Koudys. The change came with Olczyk's blessing and no blame in return; for there were few players more beloved on the roster and in the locker room than Olczyk. "There are questions that come up when that kind of thing happens," Olczyk noted. "But it was best for everyone; the team, myself. I could get back to being the kind of player I knew I was."

The 2014-15 season was a step forward for both Penn State and Olczyk on the ice. Of course there were hiccups along the way. The scene: the bathroom, in which Olczyk found himself far up north in Alaska. Penn State made the trip as part of a two-year series in the area. As they say, when you have to go, you have to go, and Olczyk had to go.

But so did the team bus. And as Olczyk left the building, the bus left the parking lot somewhere in the farthest, most northern reaches of the nation; his teammates glued to the bus window with their phones out, filming his sprint to the door with their phones.

The door didn't open. "I don't think Guy wanted to let me on," Olczyk remembered.

It was only a few more moments before the bus hit a red light and the bus driver took pity on Olczyk and opened the door. Olczyk made it on the bus, Gadowsky glaring at him all the while. Gadowsky and his staff demanded discipline from their players, even when nature called. The next two games Olczyk stayed in the lineup, but back at home he found himself scratched for four straight games. The first practice back? Olczyk had the practice of his life. "I was the best player on the ice."

Afterwards, the moment of truth finally came, and Gadowsky waited for Olczyk in his office. He ripped into his former captain. The success of the program would come from players operating at a professional level. If anything contributed to Penn State's quick rise through hockey it was the work ethic and discipline that got it there.

"I deserved it, and I knew it was coming." Olczyk said.

Back in the lineup against No. 4 UMass-Lowell it was Olczyk scoring late in a 5-3 loss.

The following night, he scored again as Penn State pulled up a historic 4-1 victory. And the story, and the scolding, were never mentioned again.

Olczyk knows that a long NHL career has likely skated on by, although his career is not yet over. He's playing for the Rockford IceHogs, an affiliate of the Chicago Blackhawks.

Sitting at home in Chicago, the city that finally became a home after a lifetime of travel, he looks at a photo. It's a shootout goal against Connecticut kept in his room. He sees it every morning, the puck slipping between the legs of the goalie, the crowd roaring, a favorite moment in a long career. A moment he earned.

Graduating so close to the promised land, it's hard not to feel a slight stab of the pain of just missing out. But having come to Penn State to lay the foundation, it's hard not to feel something else as he watches the highlights of the Nittany Lions' tournament appearance, and another word comes to Olczyk's mind as he looks at that photo.

"Pride."

NEW BEGINNINGS

2013-14

Of all the memorable moments that led up to opening night at Pegula Ice Arena, few things captured the excitement as perfectly as the Fire Marshall approving the addition of folding chairs inside the suites high above the rink.

So. Many. People. Wanted. In.

The rink's official capacity has fluctuated slightly over the years. Before the building was completed, it was slated to hold 6,000 people. By opening night, that magic number was 5,782 and during the 2016 season it topped out officially at 5,704. But on October 11, 2013, Pegula Ice Arena found room to fit 6,370 fans for the first ever game inside the brand-new building.

Capturing the buzz on paper does the night very little justice. The air was electric as fans rolled into the building, gazing at all of flashy decor, displays that showcased the Icers' history and the Division I program living in front of them, tonight, right now. Some wore Penn State jerseys, others just donned their favorite hockey team's. State College, a point where many different fan bases collided, suddenly had a team everyone could agree on.

And they did, with a passionate, deafening roar as Penn State skated onto the ice for warmups. The team was largely unknown to the fans there to root them on, but it was an eager welcome, both hoping to get to know the other better and better. There was clearly hope that the relationship would foster something special. Welcome to Hockey Valley, indeed.

That electric evening was as much about starting the journey as it was about the actual game at hand. Coaches, players, fan, administrators and the media all knew that this was the first step in a longer process. Success wasn't going to come overnight, nor was success always going to show itself in the form of wins.

But it didn't matter at that moment, and just under the feet of the fans above, Captain Tommy Olczyk said what everyone in the room was thinking.

"Thank you isn't even a big enough word for what you deserve," Olczyk said standing in front of the team, speaking to Pegula. "You not only started a Division I hockey program with your donation, it's safe to say that 95 percent of the kids in this room wouldn't be here, so not only did you help start a team here you formed a family."

For Gadowsky this moment, this speech, was as big as any in his career. There is only one chance to open a building, and the pregame speech needed to match the moment. But Terry Pegula himself stepped up first, and Gadowsky was happy to have dodged the bullet.

"Let's go out and show NCAA hockey what hard work and commitment can do for a hockey organization."

As Penn State took the ice to start the game the crowd roared again in approval. On the bench, Terry Pegula and his family looked on. And, somewhere in the midst of all the hubbub, Penn State and Army played a hockey game.

It was probably the least surprising thing of all that Nate Jensen slid to his right along the top of the offensive zone and blasted a shot through traffic into the back of the net. The first goal in the building's history came just 3:02 in regulation and the crowd erupted.

Penn State may have lost its first Division I game a year earlier, but it seemed impossible for the Nittany Lions to do so tonight. Even so, after 40 minutes of play, it was Penn State ahead by a single goal.

That was it until Curtis Loik collected a loose puck in the defensive zone and raced the other way with a shorthanded breakaway. On the bench the entire team rose to its feet, coaches on tip toes to see the final moments before the shot. And Loik finished calmly, sending the building into an even bigger frenzy up 2-0. Eight minutes later David Goodwin picked up his first goal in blue and white to all but finish the night off with just under eight minutes to play.

Eric Scheid's empty-net marker ensured that the Nittany Lions victory was never really in doubt; 4-1 as good of a score as any to start off the season. As the clock expired, the team raced to celebrate, hugs and high fives to anyone and everyone within reach. It was a small step, and in the grand scheme of a grand building just a single win. But Penn State opened its brand new home with a win and a convincing one at that.

"It was a tremendous night," said Gadowsky after the game. "The student section was definitely the first star tonight. Such a great night all around, a tremendous night for the Pegulas, Joe Battista, so many people that worked so hard to get this done.

"To come away with victory felt great. The atmosphere was tremendous right from walking out on the bench. It was a pretty phenomenal feeling."

In the following weeks, the novelty and excitement inevitably wore off and Penn State would face reality. The Nittany Lions were not short on effort, but it was evident in the early stages that Penn State was in fact a very young program. Following the emotional victory, Penn State went on to lose at Air Force twice, tie RIT and fall 5-2 to a talented Vermont team. There were plenty of positives, but the skill gap, the maturation process, were very obvious hurdles.

Perhaps the best example of Penn State trying to find its way was the environment in goal. The goalie rotation between Islanders draft choice freshman Eamon McAdam and the returning Matthew Skoff was a difficult one to predict. In this early stage, both showed potential, but neither had yet to grab the job by the horns. In turn, Gadowsky and his staff were content to bounce between the two goalies throughout the season. Early in the year, Skoff landed the majority of the starts, due in part to seniority over McAdam and a track record of success. For all of Penn State's growing pains, goaltending was not the only reason for losses.

At 1-3-1, Penn State finally got back on the winning side of things with a 5-4 victory over Robert Morris that featured a three-goal second period by Penn State. The game also continued a strong start for the speedy Eric Scheid, who scored his third of the season that evening. Sophomore Casey Bailey found the back of the net for his first of the year.

Indeed, both players would grow to become crucial pieces of the program's foundation.

Penn State followed up with a 2-1 win over Sacred Heart, managing two goals in the first period and then hanging on for dear life as Skoff made 20 saves to secure the win.

It was the span of the next six games that truly gave Penn State fans a look at how long a journey was left to take. Six games against ranked teams showcased the kind of talent the Nittany Lions were still trying to land. First came two losses to UMass-Lowell, ranked No. 13 in the nation. The opening night of the series UMass-Lowell slowly and methodically controlled the game to the tune of a 4-0 victory.

It was also then that Penn State fans began to find out about the toughness the program was trying to foster. Over the next several years, a defeat in the opening game of a series was often followed by a better and smarter effort the next night. It didn't always result in victory, but usually a much improved result.

This held true on the second night of the series as Penn State briefly tied the game at 1-1 after Scheid's fourth of the year, but a three goal opening period gave UMass-Lowell a 3-1 lead. From there Penn State pressed, but couldn't find the net despite a 16 shot second period. McAdam was up to the task with 41 saves in net, and UMass-Lowell wouldn't score again in the game. Goodwin found the net with just under eight minutes to cut deficit to one, but Penn State couldn't find the tying goal.

It was a loss, but there were moments that Penn State looked the part. Two scoreless periods by a quality opponent and a stellar performance by McAdam did not go unnoticed. All season Gadowsky would repeat a mantra that held true that night: Penn State can make progress as a team in ways that may not lead to wins on the scoreboard.

Baby steps, but important ones.

"I hate to say this, but the coaching staff looks at this [loss] as a bit of a positive," Gadowsky said after the series. "Of course you never want to lose two in a row — absolutely not. But when you look at the difference in areas we can control between yesterday and today, I look at this as a positive."

The confidence of that performance showed up the following week as Penn State took on eventual national champion Union at Pegula. Union was up 3-0 in the second period before Scheid scored an unassisted power play tally with just under 30 seconds to go in the period. Penn State scored twice more in the opening 10 minutes of the third period to tie the game. The Nittany Lions were growing up before everyone's eyes.

Maturation moments were common in the early years, but so were the near-wins. Max Novak scored with 6:50 to play to give Union a 4-3 lead and the eventual victory. Skoff was once again solid in goal with 30 saves, but it wasn't quite enough. The feeling, though, was that Penn State could pull off the shocker. Union was ranked No.15 in the nation, and despite future NHL defenseman Shayne Gostisbehere, they had looked beatable. A Saturday bounce back performance was not impossible.

Two goals in the opening seven minutes in front of a hopeful crowd confirmed that theory. Penn State looked on its way to picking up the first truly big win of the season.

Impressive player and future Union captain Mike Vecchione scored early in the second period, but Scheid's sixth of the year came just four minutes later and put Penn State back up 3-1. Forward David Glen's shorthanded goal under two minutes later energized the crowd even further.

But as Penn State would learn that night, it only takes the blink of an eye for a game to turn on its head. Two quick goals in less than four minutes by Gostisbehere pulled Union within a goal by the second period's end. Suddenly that 4-1 margin was just a 4-3 lead with Union breathing down the Nittany Lions' necks. Union tied the game 6:49 into the period, the comeback now officially complete. McAdam made 38 saves on the night for another standout performance.But the first of the heartbreakers in Pegula had arrived.

Daniel Ciampini put home a shot with three seconds to play to give Union a 5-4 victory.

The Nittany Lions were not a bad team by any stretch, but getting over the hump is a difficult task. It requires minimal mistakes, a small margin of error and a bit of luck.

Union would go on to win the national title with the combination of skill, determination and perseverance that shone through that Saturday night. Asked years later about the difference between Penn State and the best of the best, Gadowsky said that the Nittany Lions were still learning how to generate a killer instinct, and on that particular night, Union had it already.

In total, the Nittany Lions would lose 11 of the next 12 in a variety of fashions. A trip to Madison to face No.17 Wisconsin rounded out the six game stand against ranked teams and Penn State's first-ever Big Ten hockey game ended with a 7-1 defeat. The next night it was a valiant 4-3 loss.

And the trend continued. Penn State won the next game against Robert Morris 3-2 in Pittsburgh as part of the Three Rivers Classic, but the result was a date with No. 7 Boston College, a team already scheduled to travel to State College weeks later. Boston College, led by phenom Johnny Gaudreau dispatched Penn State with relative ease 8-2.

In the following weeks perhaps the most telling narrative of the season began. Penn State had gotten solid goaltending from McAdam and Skoff, but neither player had truly grabbed the job and neither had done what every good team needs of their goalie:

to steal a game. To be sure both had done more than their fair share to keep Penn State in games, but nothing was set in stone.

Hosting No.1 Minnesota back at home that seemed to slowly shift. McAdam picked up starts in six of the next seven games but no wins over that span. Penn State played Minnesota close with 3-2 and 5-2 losses. Ensuing Michigan State losses of 3-0 and 3-2 losses were the latest examples of how far the program was coming and how far it had left to go. A rematch against Boston College was far more positive, but still an eventual 3-2 defeat.

Off the ice, Penn State was taking part in a remarkable. Glen had applied to become a match for a bone marrow project and his number quite literally was called. Glen was set to miss 7-10 days following the procedure.

"The first time I found out I may have been a match was last spring," Glen said at the time. "I had to do some other blood test and then it got more serious towards November, December and then in December, I found out I'd be a match. Right now I'm just experiencing a little soreness and am worn out. Yesterday we went back to hospital and did the last round of injections. They hook you up to a machine. One needle in one arm, one coming out other and harvest what they need. Six hours hooked up to the machine, and then I was on my way."

"I was nervous," Glen said about telling Gadowsky he would miss time as Penn State tried to find its way. "At that point I didn't really know a timeline, so I was a little bit in the dark and apprehensive at first. But after talking, it was completely different. Coach was excited and on board right from the beginning and pumped for me."

According to Be The Match, the five-day PBSC donation is a non-surgical procedure and is one of two methods of collecting blood-forming cells for bone marrow transplants. A 7-10 day timetable is typical for recovery for most PBSC donors, and Glen did miss the series against Ohio State as he recovered with the blessing of his teammates and coaches.

Back on the ice, McAdam was in net for a 5-1 loss to Ohio State, and in turn Skoff finally started to see more consistent starts again. And then he struggled. A 5-2 loss to Ohio State the next night left Penn State in no-man's land when it came to the net. McAdam was getting better results, Skoff had experience, but neither were head and shoulders above the other. Enter PJ Musico, an Icers product and California kid with surfer hair, talents and personality to match, beloved by his teammates. When McAdam joined the program as one of the nation's top goalie prospects, the door seemed to close on Musico's starting career at Penn State. But with the struggles in net, Musico got the nod and McAdam wouldn't start another game for the rest of the season.

Musico's first start, an unenviable nod against a talented No.10 Michigan team was not a positive one. The Wolverines eventually took control for a 7-3 victory despite Penn State tying the game at 2-2 early in the second period as Bailey and Scheid gave the Nittany Lions a momentary glimmer of hope. Penn State felt like it had a chance, and the Nittany Lions were overdue for something good for their efforts.

That came on Saturday night.

Penn State had scored first before, so Zach Saar's tally 5:31 into the game was hardly an indication of anything special. But then Glen scored and later it was Bailey. The Nittany Lions were sitting on a 3-0 lead against the nation's No.10 team.

The team's thoughts were not far removed from the heartbreak of that Union game slipping from its grasp. With 40 minutes to go, it seemed unlikely Michigan would go down without a fight. But the Michigan goal never came. A 32-save shutout laid the foundation for an unexpected conference rivalry. Michigan looked flustered, surprised that a team with such a poor record was putting up such a fight. As Ricky DeRosa added the fourth and final goal to the scoreboard, Penn State fans cheered.

"For the coaching staff, it makes us feel good about the players buying into what we do,"

Gadowsky said after the game. "That what we do is going to pay off and yield a result like this. It's the buy-in to play like this that gives a lot of confidence in what we're doing."

In the ensuing weeks, Penn State tied Michigan State 2-2 at home and lost 2-1 the next night in another solid defensive outing. No wins, but hardly performances to forget.

Slowly but surely, things were coming together and the program could feel it.

Penn State traveled to Ann Arbor to face Michigan at Yost Arena, an old rink built in 1923 that has hosted more history than most. As far as its latest chapter, observers assumed the 4-0 loss to Penn State right in Michigan's rearview would result in a fairly competent thumping. If Michigan hadn't taken Penn State seriously before, it would now.

The game started that way, too. Michigan scored three goals in the first period with David Goodwin's lone tally keeping Penn State within reach after 20 minutes. Bailey's sixth of the year cut into the lead in the second period, but after 40 minutes a 3-2 Michigan lead still seemed safe for the Wolverines. Then a shorthanded goal by Richard tied game and stunned the Michigan crowd. But Alex Guptill got the puck past Skoff with 2:02 to go, and sent the old barn into a frenzy.

It was then that Penn Staters learned what it really had in Casey Bailey. The baby-faced Anchorage native had a rocket of slapshot and a knack for finding the back of the net. A legend of sorts was born with five seconds to play in regulation. Penn State skated with an extra attacker, and Bailey found paydirt to tie the game and send it into overtime.

Goodwin scored with less than a minute to go in overtime. Yost Arena was stunned. 3-1 had turned 3-3 then 5-4, a second straight loss to a team aspiring to be everything the Wolverines already were.

It was perhaps inevitable that Penn State couldn't repeat that upset magic on Saturday.

Michigan won 5-2 in the kind of performance meant to put Penn State back in its place.

Headed back on the road against Minnesota, the Gophers would do the same after a tough haul at Pegula, beating Penn State 5-1 and 2-1 to take a bit of the glow off the Nittany Lions.

Penn State's goalie situation continued to waver. McAdam had not removed himself from a minor doghouse social media incident, and Skoff had played the majority of the starts with a mixed bag of results. Skoff was talented, but lacked the athleticism that McAdam had and the raw talent. There was a feeling outside the program that Skoff was peaking, whereas McAdam had a far higher ceiling, but still he sat the wayside. This convoluted rotation saw little sign of calming down as Musico found himself in goal three of Penn State's final five regular season games.

The first was Penn State's 2-1 loss to Minnesota on the road, where Musico was outstanding. But then Penn State fell 4-2 and Skoff was back in the net the following night. Penn State lost 3-2 in overtime, another last second heartbreak when Wisconsin scored with just seconds to play in overtime, Penn State having tied the game with under two minutes to go in regulation.

So Musico was back starting against Ohio State in the final home series of the season. A 4-2, loss to the Buckeyes found Penn

State searching for a positive to end the year before the Big Ten tournament. A matinee crowd filled Pegula for the final moments of the inaugural season at the rink that Saturday, and they wanted a win.

A three goal first period gave fans plenty to cheer for. Penn State took a 3-1 lead into the intermission. A Taylor Holstrom goal in the final period put Penn State ahead 4-2 and the game ended with both teams coming skate to skate for a brief shoving match in the corner of the ice. Penn State headed to the Big Ten Tournament feeling good, but more importantly, it closed out Pegula Ice Arena's inaugural season the way it had opened it.

With a win.

Naturally, Penn State's first round opponent would be the same Michigan team it had given fits to all season. The Wolverines were on the NCAA Tournament bubble and needed a win to complete their postseason resume. The game itself was that of two teams with plenty of familiarity and little interest in repeating either of their respective blowouts. So it was no goals in the opening 20 minutes, and in the second it was more of the same until Taylor Holstrom found the net with 23 seconds to go in the period.

Michigan tied the game midway through the third, but neither team could find a winner.

And so, they headed to overtime.

And then a second overtime.

And with 7:15 to play in that second overtime Penn State forward Zach Saar collected a loose puck on the left circle fresh off the faceoff and rocketed a wrist-shot to win the game. The ensuing celebration would make highlight videos for years to come in a game that would later seem all too familiar en route to Penn State's Big Ten Tournament title.

Something about double overtime just works well for the Nittany Lions.

The result? A date with Wisconsin. The Badgers anticipated a tournament bid and Penn State found itself just two wins from an automatic bid of its own. All the scoring in that game would come in the second period. Curtis Loik, whose career at Penn State was a constant flash of impressive moments, put Penn State ahead 1-0, but Skoff, who was coming off a heroic 52-save performance against Michigan, was beaten twice and Penn State found itself facing an uphill battle.

On that night, the Nittany Lions couldn't quite do it. A 2-1 loss ended the season in St. Paul, Minnesota in the second round of the Big Ten Tournament. On paper Penn State finished the season 8-26-2, but there were positives to take for coaches and players looking back on the year. They had made strides. For a season that was all about taking the next step as a program, the Nittany Lions had ensured that the step was forward, not back.

PANDEMONIUM ON THE AIRWAVES

Fair or not, older brothers have a tendency to set the schedule on the weekends. They're either playing sports or maybe in a band; whatever the case may be, the age gap can often make the weekends feel more like a tour. It's family duty rather than freedom, dragged around to support the oldest in his pursuits.

For Brian Tripp, Penn State's tenured radio play-by-play star, the story was the same for him. His brother hit the field every Sunday for a meaningless athletic venture through adolescence but the Philadelphia Eagles hit the field for far more important things, a unfair twist for the younger brother.

But Tripp was as prepared as anyone can be in this case, headphone to his ears, listening to the call of legendary broadcaster Merrill Reese, living and dying on every word.

Tripp's body may have been with his family, but his mind and heart were farther away atop the stadium alongside Reese.

And he was hooked.

In this day and age, the notion of doing radio broadcasts is almost a forgotten career path.

But greats do still exist. Kevin Harlan can be heard on the airwaves, Harry Kalas and Vin Scully both elevated the medium into a world where it was their voice that carried the broadcast rather than the pictures.

In truth, the path to any success in sports media is paved with a certain amount of uncertainty in an ever-changing landscape, but at a young age those thoughts never entered Tripp's mind. All he knew was that he found his calling.

Down the road, he would make his way to Penn State, eventually calling women's volleyball games and the odd sport here or there. By the end of his education there wasn't much he hadn't done, and with a regular co-hosting job partnering with Penn State football radio announcer Steve Jones, he had the time to craft the kind of on-air confidence that helps you forget how many people are listening.

By this time, the news Penn State was creating a hockey program was common knowledge. The program would be looking under every rock to upgrade from its club standing to the best and brightest it could find to join every aspect of the operation. So Tripp applied for the radio job, and he got it after Penn State's first season at the Division I level. The program replaced longtime club announcer Steve Penstone while retaining analyst Tim King to work with Tripp.

The irony? Tripp had never called a hockey game before. His first chance came on opening night, the very first at Pegula Ice Arena. "I had a bit of a chip," Tripp remembered. "I'm not sure if that's the right way to go about it but I wanted to prove to people that I could do it." Fortunately for Tripp, on a night where there were so many memorable moments any first night struggles on his end were soon forgotten. As for King, the two warmed up in and out of the arena, the chemistry of play-by-play and analyst growing with each game.

The best radio calls are one that transcend the moment. Ones that become iconic moments in their own right beyond what was happening on the field of play. For all of the history that came in Penn State's first season at Pegula that moment didn't come from Tripp.

But in October of 2014 it did, with Penn State trailing Bentley 2-1 deep into the third period. Taylor Holstrom scored, and 16 seconds later an unassisted Eric Scheid goal gave Penn State a 3-2 lead with less than three minutes to go in regulation.

"Pandemonium at the rink!" Tripp belted out.

This call would would find itself in pregame montages, and weekly promotions. Most people don't remember the game, but anyone who has spent time around Penn State hockey can recite the call, a luxury so early in a career.

"I like the call. I think it was a fun call that captured the moment," Tripp says. "I don't ever pre-plan what I'm going to say. If you start to plan, especially with the pace of hockey, you're going to sound stupid more often than not."

Those opportunities didn't go away in the subsequent seasons. There were upsets of Michigan and Minnesota, Big Ten Tournament winners, first NCAA Tournament appearances and victories. For four seasons Tripp has made the drive across State College with his board in hand, a large sheet full to the brim with information about each player on each team. Stats, figures, trivia, everything you might need, and much that you won't.

The drive might even include a bit of rehearsal, but unlike so many sports where the storylines might be clear, the uncertainty of hockey lends itself to little more than hanging on for the ride. It's hard to ignore a simple fact : so many of Penn State's games have been riddled with history, and only one voice has carried those moments across the airwaves.

"I think it's there in the back of your mind," Tripp noted of the history in the making.

"You obviously don't want to mess up a call to win the Big Ten Championship or a game winning goal to send you to the Frozen Four, but you don't want ever want to miss the call be it early in the year or in March."

Tripp will enter this season with far more experience and confidence than he had not too long ago. Somewhere a younger brother might be pulling on his headset to listen as his older brother takes the field in his own game. And somewhere that younger brother, maybe a future broadcaster himself, will hear their calling in Tripp's voice.

Because that's just how it works.

MEANINGFUL STEPS

2014-15

Early one October evening in the hallway underneath the seats of Pegula Ice Arena, a handful of Penn State hockey players took part in their pregame ritual, kicking a soccer ball around, keeping it in the air as long as they could.

As luck would have it, the always enthusiastic Tommy Olczyk went to head the ball and instead got himself kicked in the face. Olczyk was fine, and a regretful embrace by Skoff would help nurse his teammate back to health as laughs reverberated down the passages.

The year before began with anticipation and tension, but the 2014-15 season began with far fewer stresses. Sure, excitement was still in the air, but the pressure was different than the hectic night when Pegula opened its doors for the first time.

For Olczyk, things had changed. He began the season no longer wearing the captain's C.

Patrick Koudys, a big Ontario born defenseman who carried himself well had taken over that role. Olczyk led by example and Koudys would do the same, but also figured to be in some of the team's bigger moments on the ice making big plays himself.

The exchange of responsibilities was taken well by all parties involved. Olczyk approved of the democratic transfer of power, and was even a bit relieved to relinquish a stressful role, but he was no less respected and no less a leader in the locker room. Koudys for his part, was humble, and Gadowsky appreciated both players and what they brought to the team.

"We want to establish a standard that everyone on this team can be a strong leader regardless of whether or not the individual has a letter on his uniform," Gadowsky said.

"Tommy remains an important part of our leadership core." Olczyk would in turn look for a chance to leave his mark on the season. The captainship had been an important moment in his career and his life, carving out his own place in the hockey world away from his famous father's shadow. Tommy was the very first captain in Penn State's Division I history, and nobody could take that away.

With the season set to begin against UConn, it would once again come down to the little things that would help the program move forward. This was what Gadowsky reminded his team of just moments before they took the ice: controlling the controllables and going from there.

"We're going to focus on ourselves, and create an identity," Gadowsky said. "The thing is, nobody expects that it is going to happen automatically, tonight. That we're going to be the team tonight that we're going to be in March. It doesn't work that way. We all understand there are going to be mistakes. But also, in terms of things we can do right now, those objectives, that will create our identity. They're decisions, things that we don't necessarily have to practice."

Gadowsky reminded his team that it's a decision to crash the net, to out compete their man and to avoid bad penalties; little things that would be a step forward. So it was fitting that the season began with Olczyk driving to the net late in the second period with the Nittany Lions having given up a goal minutes earlier. As a UConn defender hauled Olczyk down, the referee pointed to the center of the ice, indicating a penalty shot.

And Olczyk, who by his own admission was not an above average stick handler, snuck the puck back into the net, tying the game in a crucial moment; leadership, even without the letter on his jersey. Penn State would tie that season opener 2-2 despite Olczyk's efforts. As often was the case in the earliest stages, shooting the puck didn't always result in great chances or even goals. It was an exciting brand of hockey to watch, but it wasn't a guarantee for success.

But sometimes it worked. On Saturday night Penn State thrashed UConn to the tune of 7-1 despite scoring just one goal in the first period. A tie to open the season and then a convincing victory put the team in a good mood for the long flight to Alaska to face Alaska-Anchorage and Fairbanks on back-to-back nights.

The trip was a meaningful one for the team. While the comforts of home are appreciated, it's often the long days on the road that bring a group together. For Bailey, Gadowsky, and Alaska Anchorage transfer Eric Scheid, the trip offered them a chance to see familiar faces. For Bailey, it was a particularly special trip back home as an Anchorage native, and Gadowsky was not long removed from his tenure at Fairbanks. A trip to the Eielson Air Force Base included a tour by Penn State club hockey alumnus Maj. Joe Bassett, who was serving on the base at the time. It's a small world after all, even at the very edge of it.

Penn State tied the first game of the two-team series, but the game was forgotten when David Thompson was cut by a skate in the abdomen and lay on the ice bleeding. The cut would require 20 stitches to close, and it was a sobering reminder of how quickly an injury can happen and a career can be threatened. Thompson only missed five games, but it was enough to put a cloud over the trip for Gadowsky, who said those moments with Thompson on the ice were what he remembers about the entire trip.

The second night Alaska-Fairbanks scored twice in 27 seconds during the final six minutes of regulation. Two straight nights of blown third period leads left the team with a bitter taste in its mouth. The coaching staff wasn't overly concerned, though. The losses were inherently painful, but playing with a lead, and playing with the lead late in games is a learning process and nothing matures a team faster than mistakes.

Back in the continental U.S., that lesson would be quickly applied, Penn State rattled off four straight wins in the friendly confines of home. 3-1 and 7-1 victories over Holy Cross were welcomed by a team that felt like it could string together some convincing victories but had yet to do so. Between periods of Penn State's first win, Gadowsky entered the locker room and told the team to just "keep shelling" the goalie. The Nittany Lions ended the night with 47 shots on goal.

The second night was more of the same as Penn State played the shot-happy offense that would quickly become an identifying attribute of the program's early success. Bailey ended the weekend with his fourth goal of the year through just six games.

That particular hot streak didn't slow the next game as Bailey scored in the opening period as Penn State worked its way to a close but solid 3-2 victory over Bentley. The following night Taylor Holstrom and Eric Scheid scored 16 seconds apart to help turn

Penn State's 2-1 deficit into a 3-2 lead with just under three minutes to go in regulation.

Not only had Penn State hung on to a late lead, it had found a way to get back into a game it was close to losing. Having recently experienced two difficult losses in Alaska, it was a quick turnaround to avoid that same fate again.

In turn, this made Penn State's upcoming road series against No. 4 UMass-Lowell far more interesting. A year ago, Penn State's games against Top 5 teams, mainly No.1

Minnesota, had been valiant efforts but not much more. This season the Nittany Lions entered a similar game with a newfound confidence, solid goaltending and a consistent offensive attack. How would Penn State do against the best team it had faced all season?

And on the opening weekend of a nine game road trip away from home?

The first game of the series did little to prove Penn State was ready to take that next step.

UMass-Lowell jumped out to a 2-0 lead by the end of the first period. A Bailey goal then cut the margin to just one, but UMass-Lowell would score twice more in less than 30 seconds to yank Skoff from the net. As a result Penn State would turn to Eamon McAdam, who hadn't started in 24 games. McAdam made 17 saves in relief of Skoff and gave up just a single goal. Penn State lost 5-3 that Friday night.

On Saturday night, fans saw in net what many inside the program had. McAdam was on an upward trajectory. He came to camp one of the best pound-for-pound athletes on the team coupled with a new focus and work ethic. Like many of his teammates, the strides made between freshman and sophomore years were evident, and that was about to translate on the ice.

"The word that always came up with me was potential," McAdam said at the time. "And it almost became a very negative word in a sense because it was getting tossed around so much and it was a really heavy word and it kind of weighed on me. Because it was always potential, potential potential. And now that I've been coming more into my own, I've been maturing in more ways than one. It has become a lot lighter of a word and a lot more fun to throw around. Because now I've made it this far, and there is still potential.

So it's kind of fun and kind of cool to throw around in my mind."

Saturday night Penn State came out of the gates flexing its top line of Bailey, Holstrom and Goodwin. Bailey scored twice in just under two minutes to punch Penn State ahead 2-0 just 8:30 into the game. Scheid's goal with 19 seconds capped off an impressive 3-0 opening period.

The most impressive part of the eventual victory was Penn State's improving defense. In the first period, McAdam would be forced to make 10 saves, in the second just nine and in the third period a lowly five stops as the Nittany Lions hung on. A sweeping left to right backhanded shot by Olczyk put Penn State up 4-0 heading into the second intermission.

The 4-1 victory sent Penn State home with even more confidence in its play. Not long after those last minute miscues in Alaska, the Nittany Lions were now 6-2-2 with a win over a Top 5 team.

And up next, Michigan.

There were very few people who expected Penn State to win its first game in a return trip to Ann Arbor. It would mean three straight victories against the Wolverines and Michigan was a team loaded with talent. JT Compher, Tyler Motte, and Dylan Larkin lined a roster unlike any Penn State had faced. In the following year Compher and Motte would join up with Kyle Connor to become the vaunted CCM Line that would take college hockey by storm. And then there was the revenge factor involved. Michigan had its prior season tripped up by Penn State's upset-minded ways.

It was not terribly surprising that Michigan scored just 46 seconds into the game behind the tidal wave of emotion running through Yost Arena. McAdam got the start in net after a solid performance against UMass-Lowell, but a wrister between the dots beat him on the right side and that was all it took to open the scoring.

But this team had been learning about the value of continuing to fight. Early season lessons had stuck, and so the Nittany Lions settled down and St Louis Blue draft choice Max Gardiner made his biggest contribution of the season so far with a power play goal to tie the game late in the opening period. Twenty-two seconds later, Scheid took the puck in the defensive zone and raced past two defenders to give Penn State a 2-1 lead.

Minutes later Bailey would add another, and suddenly it was 3-1 lead at the first intermission.

Wins in Yost do not come easily and the Nittany Lions were happy with an eventual 3-2 victory. The Wolverines scored just three minutes into the final period but McAdam stopped 38 shots in the game to hold off them off and preserve the win. In victory there was celebration but Penn State did not feel great about its performance as a team.

Gadowsky's message would continue to be improving the things the team had gotten wrong: turnovers, missed chances, mental errors. He kept repeating that good results wouldn't always equate to wins, and in turn, wins weren't always the result of great play.

Penn State knew that it would have to be better the following night, something that hardly needed to be stated in the locker room after the fact. Saturday, Michigan came out firing but McAdam continued to stand tall until a three-goal second period finally overwhelmed Penn State. By the time the dust settled, the Wolverines had exacted their revenge to the tune of an 8-1 beatdown. Penn State had returned to Earth.

The very next week, Penn State traveled to Madison Square Garden to face Cornell. The Nittany Lions played well in front of a near sellout crowd, but a 3-1 defeat sent them back to Pegula Ice Arena with a loss in their first trip to perhaps the most prestigious building in the country. Back at home, Penn State was finally able to rest some tired legs at 7-4-2 on the year at the start of December.

First up was a rebuilding Wisconsin team that had handled Penn State the season prior. In the first night's meeting, Penn State rode its top line of Goodwin, Bailey and Glen to a 5-2 victory. By the time the night ended, that line had accounted for three of Penn State's five goals with each player finding the back of the net; Bailey his 10th of the season.

While still early in the maturation process as a program, the Nittany Lions had started to make good on a growing confidence that they belonged.

There were a lot of players who Penn State could point to as an example of this. Not short on confidence in their own right, Bailey, Goodwin and Holstrom were a trio expecting to score and expecting to do it against anyone they played. Bailey in particular was a player Penn State's coaching staff had long seen as a potential star, and with his production starting to climb, so too did the team's overall confidence.

In the broadest of strokes Penn State picked up just three losses over the next 13 games.

On Saturday night, the streak started as Penn State managed to beat Wisconsin again, 4-2 for its first ever home Big Ten sweep and first ever conference sweep. Victories secured in eight of the last 11 games, a few fortunate wins and a few helpful bounces to be sure, but the Nittany Lions were winning and those wins were welcome.

"It's a great accomplishment to get two wins this weekend," Gadowsky said at the time.

"The team played with poise and got the job done. There is a lot to work on over the break, but I'm proud of this team in the way it fought back from being down to keep their composure and get those goals."

The sweep also earned Penn State a ranking in the USCHO.com poll. The Nittany Lions came in for the first time in program history at No. 20. It was yet another benchmark checked off the list. While the long list of program milestones doesn't include anything about rankings, the date Dec. 16, 2014, would have fit in nicely, marking the program's first-ever ranking. Penn State would take off for the holiday break, not returning until December 29to play in a two day event again in Pittsburgh against Robert Morris and Western Michigan. The Nittany Lions lost both games.

Back in State College, Penn State had a chance to set things straight. But a talented Ohio State team arrived as Penn State got back into the thick of Big Ten play. The Buckeyes were beatable, but as the Nittany Lions had been learning all year, it would take a complete effort to do it.

On the ice Friday night, it was Skoff back in goal and Penn State came out flying, getting 18 shots on goal to Ohio State's eight. But the Nittany Lions couldn't find the back of the net. In the second period it was more of the same, but Ohio State managed a 2-0 lead heading into the middle intermission after another shot heavy period by both teams. Just 59 seconds into the third period, Ohio State beat Skoff again and Gadowsky opted to pull his heavily worked goalie in favor of Musico. Not long after the change, Ohio State would score again, all but ending the game.

And then came a seven minute span that Penn State fans won't soon forget. With just over 13 minutes to play, Bailey found the back of the net on a rebound in front of goal, slotting it past Frey's left pad. It was the 36th shot of the game on net and the first to find its way past the line.

4-1.

Two minutes later, Bailey found himself in front of the net yet again, slapping a puck past Frey while down on one knee, high on the glove side.

4-2.

David Goodwin's redirection up over Ohio State goalie Christian Frey closed in on the near impossible.

4-3.

Four-goal comebacks are by their very nature difficult to pull off. And so many times you just need a little luck to do it. So as the puck bounced through traffic behind Ohio State's net, and found its way to a wide open Bailey on the left circle, that was just enough.

Bailey rifled it home with 21.9 seconds to go in regulation.

4-4.

For the most part the overtime victory seemed inevitable. That's how these kinds of games go: a massive comeback, a massive swing in momentum, belief wrestling with disbelief. With less than a minute to play in overtime Penn State defenseman Erik Autio was seemingly tripped near center ice and the puck went the other way on a breakaway, sweeping towards the left side of the ice as the crowd stood apoplectic that a call wasn't made. But it made no difference, the puck found the back of the net, and the luck had run out. Ohio State had won.

Like the crowd, Gadowsky was livid on the bench over what appeared to be such an obvious missed call.

Following the game Gadowsky made his way to the back of the media room, watching a replay on the monitor of a television camera, he was still fuming as he made his way to the front to answer questions, opting to let the footage do the talking when it came to the call that wasn't. Penn State was beginning to feel that the team was turning a corner, things were going well in every area. To lose a game in that fashion was a difficult pill to swallow.

The next night, Penn State won 4-1 with McAdam in net behind a solid all around team performance. Scheid scored twice in a convincing win that would spark an eight game unbeaten streak. The Nittany Lions traveled to Michigan State the following week and come away with a 2-2 tie and 5-2 victory. Suddenly, Penn State was starting to find itself.

That wasn't lost on fans or the media, the Nittany Lions returned to Pegula and managed a 5-4 win and 5-5 tie against Northern Michigan. There was increasing optimism that the season might just turn into something special. In reality, there was far too much work left to be done for Penn State to have a reasonable shot at the postseason, but a 12-7-4 mark was easily the program's best so far.

If the early years of a program are about creating an identity, Penn State had found at least one character trait fairly quickly. By their January 31 meeting with No. 14 Vermont in Philadelphia, the Nittany Lions led the nation in shots per game, a 41.75 clip that was six shots per game ahead of the next best team. The result was a Top 10 scoring offense in the nation with 3.50 goals per game.

This was far from a meaningless statistic. Penn State's first NCAA Tournament team would be its own variation of these stats, relying on a relentless attack and shot count that would help create chances in the offensive zone. Where the Nittany Lions could have played a slower game, one that may have led to more victories, Gadowsky and his staff believed from the outset that their job was to develop players for the next level, and as such their offense would reflect that mindset. As a result, Penn State entered the final third of the season feeling like it could hang with anyone, and as long as the goal scoring continued there wasn't much reason to expect otherwise.

But as Penn State would learn in the second period that afternoon in Philly, the little mistakes can cost you big. The Nittany Lions went from a scoreless 0-0 game after the first period to losing 2-0 in just over two minutes.

The culprit was ill-timed penalties. Penn State was ranked in the bottom third of the nation in total penalties taken, but the Nittany Lions had a tendency to take ones at bad moments. This was one of the more challenging issues Penn State faced as it transitioned to the Division I level from club. The Nittany Lions were trying to outwork teams, and often the letter of law was interpreted in a few different ways by officials. It was a bumpy learning curve for Penn State to say the least.

The good news for Penn State was that in spite of the penalty issue the Nittany Lions were still their usual aggressive, offensive minded selves. Bailey scored his 18th of the year just 14 seconds after Vermont took a 2-0 lead.

All told, Penn State played a fairly pedestrian second period by its usual standards, just nine shots on goal. But the late goal gave the Nittany Lions plenty of momentum. Scott Conway tied the game on the man advantage at 2-2. Musico had gotten the start and played well in the two previous games against Northern Michigan, and against Vermont he continued to play well, making 33 saves by the end of the game. And while the Nittany Lions had taken six penalties, Vermont made good on just one power play all night.

Behind that effort Penn State was able to seal the deal and upset Vermont 4-2. The Nittany Lions headed back to State College with no lack of confidence, and more answers than questions across the ice. Musico continued to start and was called on in 11 of the team's final 16 games of the season.

On paper, this was a fairly innocuous change. Musico had been a reliable goaltender, and the team appeared to respond well to his play. Musico was well liked, a hard worker and had by all rights played well enough to earn those starts.

However, it planted the seeds that would lead to the departure of McAdam following his junior season. In the eyes of Gadowsky and his staff, Musico had earned the starts, and while McAdam's camp wouldn't dispute that assertion, he was by all rights a better goaltending prospect and as a New York Islanders draft choice, he was playing with the intention of bigger and better things down the road. Sitting for all but three of Penn State's final 16 games was hardly the way to go about it.

McAdam was young and maturing in his own right, Musico a veteran who had been around the block. The truth likely lay somewhere between the two camps, but the situation, for better or worse, was starting to take its toll. Nevertheless, Penn State returned home and swept Wisconsin in fairly convincing fashion, 5-2 and 4-1, to stretch the Nittany Lions' unbeaten streak to eight games.

Penn State's luck would run out on the road in East Lansing the following week. Musico and the Nittany Lions were shut out

Friday night and lost 4-3 the next night despite Bailey picking up his 20th goal of the season.

Back in State College, Penn State opted to go back to Muscio in goal against No. 15

Minnesota. The Nittany Lions were rewarded with a 33 save performance, but David Goodwin's lone first-period goal was the only for Penn State as Minnesota snuck by with a 2-1 victory. All the same, it was momentum Penn State could capitalize on. The Gophers took care of the upstart Nittany Lions in previous meetings and had enjoyed that fact.

It was not so much Penn State's existence that irked Gopher fans and college hockey fans, but it had jumpstarted a Big Ten hockey conference that in turn demolished the former WCHA. The notion that Penn State had "ruined" college hockey was a real sentiment in Minnesota even if coaches and players weren't the ones to utter those exact words. Like so many big games before and since that February, Pegula Ice Arena was ready the next night for a showdown. Two goals by Curtis Loik and Scott Conway had the Gophers on upset watch midway through the first period, the crowd roaring with each hit.

Predictably, Minnesota didn't quit, but then Conway struck again, the Basingstoke, England native pushing Penn State back up 3-1. It was penalties, again, that hurt Penn State that night and sure enough a powerplay goal just a minute after Conway's cut the lead to just one. In the third period, Penn State hung on for dear life, Musico stopping 14 shots, with a plan for himself as the clock wound down under 10 minutes.

"Just breathe."

And for 19 minutes and 20 seconds he pulled together an outstanding performance in net, but Minnesota tied with an extra attacker in the game's final moments. The crowd was stunned.

Now Penn State had to survive a five minute overtime. A tough opponent and a tough ask.

The Nittany Lions were up to the task though, swarming in the offensive zone, chasing the puck around the boards. So as Luke Juha threw a puck through traffic and into the net during a rare overtime power play, the cheer that ensued was far more than the simple euphoria of a single victory, it was the giant slain at last. And a sigh of relief from the man in net.

Of course, the relief never lasts long. Penn State would fall in Columbus 5-3 on back-to-back nights, losing Taylor Holstrom in the process to a season-ending lower-body injury. Suddenly the Nittany Lions' top line was missing one of its key pieces. And it looked as if Penn State would be missing another key piece the following year. Publically it was a business as usual for the final five games, but Penn State was preparing to lose Bailey to NHL free agency..

To the media Gadowsky said that he didn't know what Bailey would do, and Bailey would parry away questions about his future. In truth both parties knew that his time on campus was rapidly counting down. More than a few NHL services had listed Bailey as the top college free agent, and it didn't take an expert to know is stock would never be any higher, nor his age any younger.

"I just put it in the back of my head until the season is over," Bailey said, somewhat amused by the interest everyone had in his future. "My main focus is Penn State and Penn State hockey. My heart is behind this team and behind this logo and I want to bring this as far as possible and when that's over I'll look over everything and go from there."

"I not really thinking about it," He added. "I don't want to hear about everything that's going on. I think I just have to focus on my game and getting better every day."

Bailey didn't slow down any as Penn State looked to close out the home schedule in early March against Michigan, a team that the Nittany Lions took great pleasure in beating. A three-goal first period, which included Bailey's 22nd of the year, did little to change that trend. McAdam started the game in goal that night, his first start January 16th.

Conway made it 4-0, as he continued to be one of Penn State's brightest young prospects and leading freshman scorer, fifth on the team overall by the season's end, but also the team leader in penalty minutes. His eventual dismissal from the team for a violation of team rules was a tough blow to the program's immediate future, but that news wouldn't break for many more weeks. Dylan Richard's score with less than a minute to play in the period erased the Wolverines' efforts as Penn State headed to the second intermission now up 5-2. Nate Jensen's response five minutes after Michigan's third of the night ended any comeback hopes and the Nittany Lions won with an eventual 6-3 final score.

The next night Penn State marked its final game at home with a Senior Night celebration that was capped off by Musico getting the start in goal. It was a bold move, if only because McAdam had played well the night before, and the Nittany Lions were looking to end the season on the strong note. But Musico made 31 saves on the night in spite of a JT Compher hat trick, and Penn State won 4-3, Conway picking up his 10th of the season in the process.

Despite the high notes, the latter third of Penn State's season was a reminder of where the program still had to go. The Nittany Lions headed to Minnesota the following week and managed just two goals while giving up 11. Penn State headed to the Big Ten Tournament missing Holstrom and having won three of the season's final 10 games. At 18-14-4, this had been the Nittany Lions' best season by far, but it was clear that the gap between the top of the Big Ten and Penn State was still wide.

That was evident when Penn State found itself out of the Big Ten Tournament following a 3-1 loss to Ohio State. The Buckeyes jumped out to a 2-0 lead in the first period and leaned on goaltending to backstop an eventual 3-1 victory. The good news was that the Nittany Lions would return much of the team's core. The bad news was that Bailey would sign with the Toronto Maple Leafs, Conway was dismissed and Musico and his fellow seniors graduated, but the team wouldn't look too different despite the departures.

Most importantly, there was talent on the way. Andrew Sturtz headlined a group of incoming freshman that marked the best recruiting haul to date for the program. A small but important step forward yet again.

And the season ahead would be the best one yet.

THE VOICE OF THE RINK

Sitting at the surface of the ocean you can fasten a string tightly to each side of the wall of a submarine; the line taut like tightrope walker's small grasp on the very edge of life.

But as you slowly descend into the ocean, the rope becomes more and slack, the crushing forces of the water above compressing the sides of the boat. It groans and creaks with strain, but at the right depth there is no unpredictable danger. It is physics, after all.

Nevertheless, a submarine is undoubtedly near the top of the list of unpleasant ways to die in the service of one's country. The structural failure of the boat would be a near-instant crush. If not that, then perhaps an engine failure, stuck in some awful purgatory of awaiting rescue in a metal tube some unknown depth below the ocean.

These dangers are –while certainly real—not necessarily in the forefront of the minds of those who serve, if for no other reason than the likelihood of those unspeakable misfortunes is quite small. But for Rodney Martin and his fellow crew members of the USS Sand Lance, it was just another part of the job.

■ ■ ■

Long before Martin ever found himself deep underneath the ocean he was growing up in eastern PA, taking in all the hockey you could ask for. There were Flyers' games and Hershey Bears showdowns alike. It's an unavoidable part of eastern Pennsylvania sports culture.

But like everyone else growing up, the step after high school was a challenging one.

Martin chose the service, because sometimes that's simply the calling, and for the next six years he used a math intensive background and his talents and interests in mechanical engineering to help run and operate a 292-foot Sturgeon attack class submarine stationed out of Charleston, South Carolina.

Martin spent his work time helping set course and speed for the Sand Lance in addition to the somewhat important job of making sure the nuclear reactor was working in addition to the steam elements of the engine; as you might imagine, failure somewhere deep in the ocean is not an optimal outcome.

The rest of the time? That was dedicated to hockey talk. Submarines deep beneath the ocean's surface don't lend themselves to much alone time, and for Martin and friends nothing passed the time better than discussing the hockey a few hundred feet above their heads.

So it was only natural that as Martin found himself at Penn State working at the Applied Research Laboratory, he would join the hockey management association his very first week in town. The group was responsible for the behind-the-scenes backbone of the Icers organization. They handled everything from programs to in-game music to goal announcements.

Like all good journeys, Martin's didn't start where it finished, having begun with just the in-game music at Greenberg Ice Pavilion. He had grown up around music and had an older brother working in the radio industry helping nurture an interest in the DJing process.

But it didn't stick. As luck would have it, Martin ended up working one night as a stand-in, announcing goals over the speakers as they rolled in. Coach Joe Battista remarked that someone needed to take over the role, and looking to help in any way he could, Martin volunteered for the job. The rest, as they say, is history.

Nearly a decade after Martin got to town, Penn State announced the creation of the Division I program. There were absolutely no guarantees that he would make the trip with the team to Pegula Ice Arena. Many people saw their volunteer work inherited by new faces and new names as the program took the next step. Martin knew he could be replaced.

So he met with Penn State's marketing director and later Battista, hoping against hope that they would keep him on board. Martin had an ace in the hole too -- Battista liked him. As they both grew the Icers, program Martin helped host a weekly Icers television broadcast on CNET and while he doesn't admit it, Battista claims that the first time he heard the words "Hockey Valley" they had come from Martin's mouth.

So keeping Martin around was Penn State's plan all along.

When Penn State opened Pegula Ice Arena nothing was all that new to Martin. He had been the public address announcer for nearly two decades now. The horn sounded, the assists registered and the goal announced. It's not rocket science.

But it was opening night, and there was history to be made. Everything in fact, was history. Everything was a first. And as Nate Jensen's shot from the point navigated through traffic and into the back of the net, it was Martin's first chance to shine.

And he did, thanks to a few mental reps on the drive over, a few extra practices of just getting all the words out in the right order yet again. Nothing about what he was doing was new, but nobody wants to mess up that moment.

From there on out, Martin has continued to be a staple of game day at Pegula. He arrives early, a coffee and a long walk around the concourse before the doors open. He doesn't have to worry about the music anymore, but he still listens, taking in all the sights and sounds along the way.

It hasn't been a perfect ride. In a last second loss to Boston College, Martin slammed his headset to the ground and received what he would describe as a "stern talking to." He did it again after Penn State's overtime loss to Minnesota in 2017, and he was inconsolable.

The journey to the top hasn't been easy, but nearly two decades ago it would have seemed impossible.

So sitting in front of a bowl of soup in downtown State College, wearing a Firefly shirt, it's a reminder of how far everything has come. From somewhere deep below the ocean's surface to high above the crowds roaring as Penn State takes the ice.

Stirring his food, Martin says, "I'm blessed."

SO CLOSE YET SO FAR

2015-16

Entering the 2015-16 season, Penn State had a problem.

The departure of Casey Bailey coupled with the graduation of players like Taylor Holstrom, Patrick Koudys and Nate Jensen left a void to be filled. Penn State's heralded top line was down to just David Goodwin. The Nittany Lions would also be without Scott Conway, dismissed for a violation of team rules over the summer.

Penn State faced a straightforward issue with scoring. The Lions exited the previous season ranked fourth in the nation in scoring by senior players, although Bailey alone accounted for a good number of them. Penn State had ground to make up.

Penn State's coaching staff knew the team would need to get back to the kind of balanced scoring it envisioned in the first place. There were talented players returning, and new talented faces headed to campus, so this team would rely on its depth, not the singular star power of a few players. That was the plan.

It made sense that players and coaches unanimously agreed to name David Glen captain.

Reliable on both ends of the ice and an outstanding example away from it, Glen was the steady hand on the helm Penn State would need.

"He was a unanimous choice for sure, as well as the coaching staff's. Number one, you want someone who represents your program and your university," Gadowsky said when it was announced. "The way he plays, you know he has the overtime game winner in our first Division I win, and he's also a guy who very quickly gave up playing games to donate bone marrow for someone in need. And that's the kind of person we need. He's an excellent student and selfless for the greater cause and the community or anyone who needs it. I'm proud to call him our captain at any time. He fits us great."

On opening night that plan worked to perfection as Penn State blew past Canisius 6-1. By the end of the night five different Nittany Lions had scored and Glen found the back of the net twice. A solid 27-save performance from goalie Eamon McAdam, now a junior, was not to be overlooked. McAdam had always been an excellent athlete, but over the summer his maturation continued both physically and mentally, beating out his teammates running stairs and in the weight room. The graduation of PJ Musico opened the door for McAdam or Skoff to grab the starting job. Most onlookers assumed that this new McAdam would earn the starting job on a more regular basis. Time would tell.

The Nittany Lions had to wait a week before a highly anticipated series against Notre Dame. Notre Dame would join the Big Ten for hockey two years later, reportedly tired of travel outside of their region. The Big Ten would give Notre Dame not only plenty of nationally relevant teams to face, but a much more palatable travel schedule.

Notre Dame came into Friday night's game firing away and beating Skoff three times in the first period. Skoff wasn't sharp, but as was often the case that season, the deficit was a group effort. The scoreline chased Skoff from the net in the third period as he was replaced by fan favorite Chris Funkey, and the night ended at a disappointing 7-4.

Heading into the second night of the series, Penn State faced a difficult challenge. A former USHL teammate of McAdam's in Iowa, Notre Dame goalie Cal Petersen had quickly become one of the best young goalies in the nation.

Petersen also presented a difficult challenge for a Penn State offense that was often high on shots, but not equally high on quality chances. The Nittany Lions' shoot-first offense had been an effective tactic each season, but a good shot-blocking defense coupled with outstanding goaltending had stifled Penn State in the past. The Nittany Lions lived on rebounds and crashing the net, so Petersen's reliability posed a problem.

Nonetheless Penn State put five pucks past him, winning 5-3. It was a David Thompson goal that helped Penn State avoid another night of early quick strikes from Notre Dame.

Penn State's second period was the pinnacle of what the offense could do when momentum was on its side. Notre Dame took a 2-1 lead, even as the Nittany Lions poured on the offense with an apparent goal taking the wind out of Notre Dame's sails after such a dominant opening period. Less than a minute later, freshman Chase Berger tied the game. Then Marsh picked up his third of the year. And 47 seconds later, Ricky DeRosa scored, a one-goal deficit turned into a two-goal lead in two minutes and 21 seconds. Notre Dame would get a goal, but couldn't beat McAdam and

Penn State's defense. An empty net goal by Curtis Loik finished the 5-3 victory.

It was a solid confidence boost early in the season for a team learning the ropes with a young corps of freshmen and without familiar faces of seasons past. Penn State then beat AIC in fairly routine 8-3 and 5-3 victories that continued to showcase the potential of an increasingly high powered offense backed up by talent.

Yet in the subsequent series against St. Lawrence, the complete opposite would happen.

The first night ended in a tie, despite 50 shots on goal. The following night Penn State managed *only* 38 shots on goal and two third period goals for a 4-2 loss.

"We escaped tonight for sure," St. Lawrence coach Greg Carvel said after the first game of the series. "I thought the first 30 minutes were pretty lopsided. We got outclassed for 30 minutes. Luckily we were outstanding on the penalty kill with the seven penalties we had to kill off." All things considered it was a positive weekend for a team eager to learn and eager to improve.

Up next, a Niagara game resulting in a 1-1 tie, but the Nittany Lions continued to feel like they were growing. They also just had to stay the course.

Penn State's patience paid off. The Nittany Lions blew out Sacred Heart 8-2, as Berger and Marsh registered their sixth and fifth goals, respectively. The biggest surprise so early in the year was the Penn State freshmen contributing in such high volume. Berger in particular had shown an unexpected nose for the net. This group was expected to elevate Penn State's overall talent pool over the span of months and years, not weeks. Berger's streak continued the following night, as he scored twice more en route to an eventual 3-2 victory.

Penn State headed to Anchorage the following week, the final leg of a multi-year series scheduled to get the likes of Casey Bailey in front of his hometown. Without Bailey, the nostalgic aspects of the trip were gone, but after tough results the last time the team went to Alaska, a 5-2 victory and a 1-1 tie were perfect souvenirs for the long flight home.

If Penn State hockey has a second home it could argued that the Wells Fargo Center in Philadelphia is it. The Nittany Lions played their fair share of games both in Pittsburgh and the City of Brotherly Love, but by now it was easy to tell where that second fan base lived.

Philadelphia and its Penn State alumni had embraced the Nittany Lions fully; a single game against Vermont in late November was enjoyed by over 9,000 ecstatic fans packing in to see Penn State's increasingly potent offense take the ice. The Nittany Lions rolled through the Catamounts 4-0 to improve to 8-2-3 on the year.

Zach Saar —who made a career of trips to the penalty box-- scored first on the power play.

Dylan Richard did the same in the final three minutes of the second period to put Penn State ahead 2-0. On the opposite end of the ice McAdam put up the kind of goaltending effort Flyers' fans wanted for their own team, stopping 16 shots to keep his shutout alive.

Chase Berger's ninth goal of the year soundly shut the door as McAdam continued to hold, preserving the shutout. Richard's second goal in the game's dying seconds finished off the night to a loud ovation as Penn State headed back to State College.

What awaited the Nittany Lions was its best test to date, a Michigan State team that, like Notre Dame, had some of the nation's best goaltending. Jake Hildebrand had slowed Penn State the previous season, and the Spartans won three of the four meetings with some ease. This series would serve as a benchmark for the progress of Penn State's offense so far.

Walking into the locker room moments before the game, Gadowsky placed his hands in his pockets and took a few steps past the door. He looked to his right, players dressed and waiting for him, the same to his left. "We're ready," Gadowsky quipped, and then returned the way he came.

The opening period was an offensive salvo by Penn State with 13 shots on goal, but Michigan State was not far behind. Andrew Sturtz scored first, unassisted, just 10 seconds into the second period. The goal was Sturtz's seventh of the year. The smiling freshman out of Buffalo was just another member of Penn State's exploding freshman class. During his recruitment, Penn State had seen him drive to the net, and if any player personified Penn State hockey's aggression and attacking style of play it was him.

David Goodwin followed up with a goal of his own as Michigan State tried to survive a 17 shot second period. Minutes later, Sturtz scored again before assisting on defenseman Vince Pedrie's goal. It was a three point period for Sturtz, a four goal period for the Nittany Lions. Hildebrand didn't take the ice for the third period.

Michigan State found the back of the net twice, but the damage was already done. Penn State had won against a team it had struggled with at nearly every turn in the past. A 4-2 final said it all. Inside the locker room, the excitement following the game was palpable but there was the undeniable truth that one win wasn't going to turn the tide for good.

If Penn State hadn't cracked Michigan State before, it certainly did the following night as Eric Scheid scored twice in the opening 3:50 to give the Nittany Lions a 2-0 lead right off the bat. A goal by Ricky DeRosa pushed Penn State ahead 3-0, and the crowd stood and cheered as the Nittany Lions left the ice. The game wasn't over, but it certainly felt that way.

The rest of the night was more of the same, as Penn State fired 40 shots on goal while McAdam had to fend off just 28. By the end of the night, the Nittany Lions were ahead 6-1, a total of 11 goals against a team that had given Penn State fits not 12 months before.

"I thought Hildebrand handled the puck really well, and we couldn't get anything going in the first period," Gadowsky said after the game. "We were fortunate to have some bounces go our way in the second period."

This marked a significant moment in the program's history. Wins against AIC and the like were good, but convincing victories against Michigan State and Vermont were meaningful benchmarks. These wins weren't by mistake. They were the result of good play. The Nittany Lions crept back into the rankings, on their way to their highest ranking to date.

For a team that never really lacked confidence, winning certainly didn't hurt any. Penn State rolled past Princeton 6-3 in an nostalgia game for Gadowsky at Pegula. Fans, mainly students, having fun at the Tigers' expense with signs like "Guy likes us more."

Before the Big Ten schedule came calling there was a trip to face Robert Morris in the Three Rivers Classic. A two-day tournament featuring four teams.

The problem for Penn State's staff was getting the team in the "now" for that trip against a Robert Morris team that continued to take quite a bit of joy in knocking the new kids down a few pegs. Whether it was their own enthusiasm or Penn State looking ahead to Minnesota, the Colonials did just that. By the time the Nittany Lions blinked they were behind 4-1. Robert Morris then made it

6-3 with just over two minutes to go in the game, and Richard's goal made it a 6-4 in the game's final seconds.

Fortunately for the Nittany Lions, they found themselves playing Clarkson the following day and a 5-1 victory was largely a formality. At 12-3-3 on the year, Penn State was hardly struggling, but the trip was definitely a lesson in paying attention to the here and now.

It is rare for games to match their hype. Or live up to their potential. But this one, an early January meeting, did all that and more. Minnesota rolled into town the following week with no shortage of talent, and Penn State had no shortage of confidence in its ability to beat the Gophers. Penn State was an upstart Big Ten hopeful, Minnesota was struggling more than expected with just eight wins. But still plenty of skill.

A rare first period saw Penn State outshot by its opponent, the middle 20 minutes were a battle. If there was a moment in the season that McAdam began to truly show his NHL potential, it could be found here; somewhere around 8 p.m. in early January of 2016, where he already had 31 saves to his name. Often great goaltending can be all for naught, but Zach Saar collected the puck in a net mouth scramble to put Penn State up 1-0. Four minutes later, Sturtz barreled down the ice to do the same, sweeping from right to left, putting Penn State ahead 2-0. Minnesota found a way to beat McAdam just 1:39 into the final period and then again to tie the game. Neither goalie would relent at that point.

And so it was overtime.

For three minutes and 57 seconds, it looked like the game was headed to a shootout for the extra point. But then Erik Autio, Penn State's quiet Finnish defenseman found Tommy Olczyk behind the net and Olczyk funneled the puck to the top of the offensive zone to Pedrie. Pedrie, ready for the puck, lined up his shot, slammed it through traffic and scored. Penn State had won 3-2.

The goalies had made a combined total of 76 saves with 34 more shots getting blocked on their way to the net. The concern, of course, was that final shot total for Minnesota.

McAdam had put forth a heroic effort, and was nearly not enough. It stood to reason that Penn State might not be so lucky two nights in a row.

The Nittany Lions weren't. Following a big night, it was Skoff, not McAdam in net and on the losing end of a 7-1 blowout loss. The defeat was hardly all on Skoff. Penn State gave up two short-handed goals in the game and an empty net tally. If Minnesota was looking for a moment to help turn their season around, it couldn't have been much better opportunity than that Saturday night. The silver lining for the defeat was the continued emergence of freshmen defensemen Pedrie and Kevin Kerr. Pedrie would be outpaced in goals scored by freshmen defensemen by just two other players. His point total was seventh best among NCAA newcomers by the end of the year.

As for Kerr, coaches had seen his abilities with the puck at both ends of the ice and knew his potential, but then a light switch flicked on. He changed and, with him the team. Kerr was quickly becoming an impact player on both ends of the ice, well ahead of schedule.

His numbers weren't eye popping, but his skills were undeniable. By the end of the year, Kerr would finish 12th among freshmen defensemen with 17 points.

All of this was a part of a new but important wrinkle to Penn State's style of play. In the past the team had been stocked full of more traditional defensemen; a stay-at-home style of play that didn't lend itself to much in the way of the offensive zone. But the game at all levels had been changing, and defensemen were becoming a bigger part of the attack.

The era of Chris Pronger frames and brute force was being replaced, in part, by a finesse skillset. So Penn State recruited that way, and was ahead of the curve in that regard since Gadowsky's scheme lent itself naturally to aggressive defenders.

"Growing up I always used to make those moves," Kerr said of his movement with the puck. "Maybe a little head fake and move the opposite way things like that. It just comes with being confident, I've always had the confidence that I could do it, but it comes with having the confidence showing that I can do it out there. It has been awesome. All year we've been really active, whether it's pinching down the wall or getting into the zone rather than a system where we may not have as much leniency to move around. So the offensive system that we play definitely fits the style of our defensemen."

It didn't always work to perfection. Penn State won a back-and-forth 4-3 overtime affair the following week against Wisconsin that never needed to be that close. The Nittany Lions threw 54 pucks on net as the Badgers managed to get 22 on Skoff. It was as lopsided as it gets, but less than a minute into overtime David Goodwin scored the winner. The next night, Penn State won 4-1 despite each team giving up a shorthanded goal and each team rocketing nearly 40 shots on net; McAdam picking up the win in the process.

As a result, the Nittany Lions sat at 15-4-3 on the year just past the season's midway point. It was by far the best start in the program's history, yet the team was clearly still a work in progress. The confidence, the goalscoring and the goaltending were all accounted for, but it was about to get far harder.

The Wisconsin game also started a span of 12 games on the road in the final 15 of the season. The Nittany Lions could win at home in front of one of the best crowds in the sport, but winning on the road, especially in the Big Ten, was a challenge time and time again. That challenge didn't go away as Penn State hit the road to face Ohio State. The Buckeyes had only won six games, but in the Big Ten the weakest teams on paper often put up the biggest fight.

That was apparent as both teams combined for 70 total shots on goal when the game entered overtime. In fact it was Ohio State holding on to a slim one-goal, lead as Kerr scored to tie the game with just under five minutes to play in regulation. Midway through overtime, Marsh won the game for Penn State, but the clear message was that the Nittany Lions had gotten away with one once again.

They didn't the following night. The Buckeyes jumped out in front and never looked back. By the time Penn State finally scored, Ohio State was already ahead 3-1 early in the third period. It was a stark reminder that no matter the team and no matter the night before, nothing comes easy in the Big Ten.

But nothing was a better reminder of that than the upcoming series against Michigan. In previous years Penn State had been fortunate. Michigan had been very good team, but perhaps not the elite level of their past. The Wolverines were talented but hadn't always taken the young upstart Penn State program seriously enough. And in turn, Penn State was able to find ways to win.

This Michigan team coming to Pegula was a different animal altogether. The vaunted CCM line of Kyle Connor, JT Compher and Tyler Motte was perhaps the best in college hockey. It was the kind of line that will go unmatched for years. The CCM line was the best of what the sport could offer, and it had the stats to back it up, with all three players in the conversation for the Hobey Baker Trophy, college hockey's Heisman. By the season's end, the CCM line would see Connor and Motte with over 30 goals each and Compher racking up nearly 50 assists in the regular season. Simply put, a line unlike anything Penn State had ever seen.

"It's not a matter of changing," Gadowsky said of adjusting to their opponent's tempo.

"But we certainly are aware of the fact that often we talk about controlling our tempo to have teams match us. I'd be lying if we said ... 'The goal is to make Michigan match us.'

We understand how they play." On top of that Michigan entered the game No. 6 in the nation, Penn State sitting at No. 15. "We have a really big game Thursday," Gadowsky said. "That's all we're talking about right now."

Penn State fans made their way to Pegula as early as the doors would open, energized and ready to watch what was about to unfold. By the time the game began the building was as charged and excited as it had ever been. Meanwhile, Michigan warmed up, comfortably preparing, unfazed by the commotion on the other side of the glass.

For the first eight minutes, the crowd was invested in each hit, every shot. All of that evaporated as Motte scored nine minutes in. The Nittany Lions weren't going to go down without a fight, though and after years of getting upset, neither were the Wolverines. By the end of the first period, each team had scored twice. Shots were 13-11 in Penn State's favor. The only good news was that the Nittany Lions were getting shots on goal, and if the Wolverines had any weakness, it was in net.

But Michigan scored three times in the second period, all from the CCM line. Tommy Olczyk's goal late in the period did just enough to keep a 5-3 margin within reach, but it was clear who the better team was. By the end of the night, Skoff had been pulled and Funkey entered the game, stopping a breakaway chance moments later. Penn State was a much better team than it had been, but lost 7-3 all the same. Michigan played to send a message, and it had.

Two days later they would face off again, this time at Madison Square Garden as part of a hoops and hockey doubleheader pitting Penn State and Michigan against each other.

There was a hope that the series on the court and the series on the ice would end the day a split. A crowd of over 13,000 largely made up of Penn State faithful from the New York area, hoped for it too.

Once again Michigan scored first, and Penn State answered.

And once again the teams entered the first intermission deadlocked.

And once again the CCM line broke the tie 15 seconds in the second period with a shorthanded goal.

But the Nittany Lions didn't fold. Sturtz and DeRosa scored and the crowd erupted.

During Penn State's rise, Gadowsky and players had been asked time and time again what made great teams so good, what Penn State was still trying to get good at. The answer was a killer instinct. Finding a way to win games that should be won, and getting back into games when momentum hits. The Nittany Lions could do it at times, but to do it consistently was a key, and they didn't have it just yet.

But Michigan did, and a four-goal third period with the Nittany Lions struggling to keep up showed how far apart the Wolverines and Penn State were. Sure, Penn State had picked up a few upsets, but Michigan was a team with purpose and a team with that killer instinct. The losses were a reminder for coaches and players, and a lesson that a young team learned. In hindsight, both parties would say it prepared them for their successes in 2016. If a season of club play had laid the foundation for the first season of Division I play, then 2015 was a foundation of experiences for 2016 and beyond.

Asked what the team had to do different, Gadowsky was to the point. "Nothing," he said.

"We just have to do the same things better." Of course it didn't get any easier. Penn State traveled to Minnesota the following week and lost 4-1 in the process. Awaiting the next game inside a somber locker room looking at a tough night in a tough conference in a tough building, Gadowsky spoke.

"If there is anyone in here who wants to go out there and keep this thing close, stay right here." He said. "But if you want to go out and play your ass off for 60 minutes and play hard and have a great performance and come out with a win, then go ahead."

No one stayed behind.

40 minutes later the teams sat deadlocked at 3-3.

It was a moment to bounce back, a moment to make good on all the progress and steal one on the road. "You know what? It's 3-3 in Mariucci," Gadowsky said to his team at the second intermission, shrugging his shoulders. "We haven't won here yet, twenty minutes left. I'll take that any day boys. No passive mistakes. Not one passive mistake.

We're all going to make mistakes in this game, guarantee it. But they better be because we're going balls out for the boys. Right? So let's play to win. We're not playing to skate for 3-3, we're skating short shifts for 20 minutes, balls out to win this game. Okay, boys?"

Sixteen minutes later, Gadowsky got his answer when Saar slid through the offensive zone to his right, firing a shot through traffic. Then with 11 seconds to play Kenny Brooks scored, and the win, Penn State's first at Minnesota, was final.

The momentum was obvious, too. Penn State faced Michigan State and proved that the progress was real en route to a 6-1 win and 2-2 tie. At home, the Nittany Lions continued to roll with a 6-1 win over Ohio State. Then Penn State hit a wall. Ohio State won 7-4 on Senior Night at Pegula with Skoff making his final start in goal for the Nittany Lions.

McAdam and Skoff had continued their rotation, but it was McAdam who had been in net for some of the season's biggest wins.

Penn State won 2-1 at Wisconsin, and then lost 4-3 the following night. And at the close of the year it was no better. A trip to Ann Arbor for the CCM's final series of the season had little in the way of a friendly climate. 7-1 and 6-1 victories for the Wolverines are hardly high points in a historic season for Penn State.

So the Nittany Lions hobbled into the Big Ten Tournament hopeful to put together some magic. 0-0-0 in the tournament but 20-12-4 on the season, hitting the 20-win mark for the first time ever. And for a change, Penn State knew who would be in goal for the postseason well in advance. Hopeful for good results and a bit of experience if the NCAA Tournament came calling, McAdam was slated to start.

"We looked down the road and no matter what, best case scenario, someone's going to have to play two games in a weekend, so we want someone to have that experience,"

Gadowsky said early in the week. "We want to do all we can right now to get a bye."

Fortunately for Penn State the tournament had been a favorable venue in the past and a 4-1 lead against Wisconsin didn't change that for Penn State. The Badgers struggled with McAdam as he made 35 saves. The 5-2 victory set up a date with Michigan in the second round, but Penn State was thoroughly outclassed by the Wolverines' top line. The game never really competitive and the Nittany Lions were crushed 7-2, despite 40 shots.

And so Penn State's season ended somewhat unceremoniously. McAdam would sign with the Islanders, both camps in a much better place than years ago but McAdam hoping for the volume of starts and opportunities that a professional career would bring. It was a blow to Penn State's goaltender corps with Skoff graduating, but with highly touted netminder Peyton Jones on the way, there was cautious optimism it could be remedied.

Despite the sour ending, Penn State's season made the biggest and most meaningful strides in the program's history. The roster was as deep as it had ever been, the games as competitive and the Nittany Lions looked the part of a Big Ten program rather than hopeful additions to the college hockey landscape.

With talent headed into the program and a young corps of players returning, there were plenty of reasons to assume more progress would come the following season as well.

Little did the Nittany Lions realize what lay ahead.

COPS, STICKS, AND SKATES

There is something of an inherent toughness that comes with living in Michigan. The state, two separate landmasses, is almost entirely surrounded by water. But these waters aren't a luxurious retirement getaway.

Four of the five Great Lakes relentlessly pound away with lake effect snow and piercing cold winds. The average high in January is below freezing, according to U.S. Climate Data. There is no place to hide.

Which probably explains why so much of the state has turned to hockey. It's a tough sport played in the cold. You may as well make the best of it. And if anything, the rinks might just be warmer than outside, assuming you're lucky enough to play inside. The Detroit Red Wings offer hockey legends in a town that epitomizes a changing nation, one of the nation's toughest cities in one of its toughest states.

It's hard a thing to ignore, the allure of an iconic team in a state that loves the sport so much. Adam Sheehan grew up around the rinks, eventually attending Western Michigan, a two-hour drive from Detroit; close enough to justify the occasional trip to see those legends take the ice.

But hockey itself wasn't in cards for Sheehan, or at least it didn't appear to be. At Western Michigan he majored in criminal justice hoping that his work would eventually lead him to one of the nation's great law enforcement acronyms, be it the CIA, the FBI, or the NSA.

He began in Phoenix, Arizona which at the time was one of the fastest growing cities in the country. In turn, it needed law enforcement, so Sheehan arrived in a place quite unlike the cold he had grown up with. The average temperature in Michigan, is just 48.2 degrees. In Arizona? Seventy-five degrees.

But hockey never really left Sheehan. He was still around rinks; beer leagues, pickup games. He wasn't great, but he could hold his own, and it got him invited to his fair share of games. During that time, he got to know the equipment staff in Phoenix. Support staff never seem to leave the arena. There is laundry to finish, skates to sharpen, sticks that need a specific curve. It isn't glamorous, but it's crucial. And Sheehan wanted in.

Eventually he got what he wanted, and was added to the game night equipment staff doing the dirty work with visiting teams. For Sheehan it was something of a baptism by fire into the NHL. He got to know visiting teams, building rapport with players from across the league on the back of a lot of hard and often unpleasant work.

From Phoenix, Sheehan found his way to Carolina, but the stint was short lived as the NHL lockout ended any sense of security. That's a feeling Sheehan wouldn't forget. It was back to the warmth of Arizona after a short stay at Sacred Heart.

Consider the unpredictability of life. As Sheehan looked to return to friends and family, he blew up the phones of the Red Wings' equipment staff, hoping there would be an opening on the staff some day. And in 2008, there was.

"I got a call on a Thursday that the job had opened up and I got the call that night and they said 'be there Monday.' and I'm in Phoenix. I had a dog and basically packed up and was gone the next day." Sheehan remembers.

Of course a call that ends with "Be here by Monday" upends a life. Sheehan packed as much as he could muster into the car and drove to Detroit. His parents, out of country, got a call that he was on his way, crashing at their house in the interim.

That first night in Joe Louis Arena was a memorable one and a full-circle moment from the days when Sheehan had watched games from the other side of the glass. Thankfully for Sheehan, he was a familiar face for more than a few Red Wings, who were a year removed from a Stanley Cup championship, and saw him working those long nights in the visiting locker rooms back in Phoenix.

Professional sports is a business, and for the better part of a decade, Sheehan had seen everyone on every level come and go. A coach could get fired, and the next day Sheehan could find himself without a job. It's an unstable way to live, and a risky one for someone hoping to settle down.

The answer to that problem is an unexpected one in the hierarchy of sports. College jobs started to become to coveted spots in the profession. So as he did earlier in his path, Sheehan blew up phones, knowing that Penn State might be that next job, and one that would give him the security he was looking for. And it was.

"The [college] job is the same," Sheehan said. "But you've got a life and you're not in a situation where if someone leaves or gets fired, I don't have to worry about my job. It's a lot safer at this level. One of the things I've seen over the years is NHL guys trying to get these jobs. If you can find a school that has a good team and has good facilities, those are the jobs NHL guys are trying to get into and spend their careers here."

Consider the unpredictability of life. Suddenly, he was Happy Valley bound. It was an interesting time to join a program too since the building hadn't been yet been constructed.

Sheehan was in a cold sweat when considering the logistical nightmare that was Greenberg Ice Pavilion, but the promises of Pegula were too much to pass up, and a small hand in the design was an interesting moment in his career. He helped retool lockers during the design process, ones that wouldn't have quite worked as hockey players would need them to.

Nothing is quite as easy as it looks. Player want their skates cut a certain way, their sticks curved a certain style. Where the women's teams get prototype sticks in the offseason to play with, Sheehan avoids that with the men's team as another variable players believe impacts their game. In total there are about five different skate shapes on the team, but the goal is simple: to keep it simple. Even if that means cutting a skate one way, and telling them it was cut how a player wanted it.

"What they don't know can't hurt them," Sheehan says with a smile. "Guys are saying they need this kind of profile like the bigger guys have Anaheim, and I'm like, 'No you're not Ryan Getzlaf'"

The result is something of a dream scenario. When the Sabres and Blues played a preseason game at the rink, NHL players could be seen filming the facility. Brian Gionta, who knew Sheehan from his time in the NHL, noted how Pegula was better than a good chunk of the league. And Sheehan knew it, putting everything in its place along the way.

His hope is that when the day comes and he's no longer equipment manager at Penn State, the next one will look at the setup and nod.

"When I'm not here some day down the road I want the next guy to come in and say "This is good. This is how it should be?"

CAUTIOUS OPTIMISM

2016-17
Pt. 1

"Is everyone in here?" Gadowsky asked, surveying the locker room, scratching his head and searching for the right words.

For most coaches those words would have been hard to find because Penn State was trailing No. 1 Denver 5-2 after two periods. The comeback trail was a daunting one to say the least. This seemed out of reach. The odds were simply too great.

What Gadowsky had learned over the past several months was that this team always seemed indifferent to the odds. Penn State's ability to ignore those odds put the Nittany Lions just one win away from the Frozen Four. And so the unexpected and unlikely had become ordinary for this team. Maybe one more bit of magic was not too much to ask.

Even so, there was no need to overlook the obvious. This wasn't going to be easy.

"The truth is, your whole year has been improbable. That's the truth," Gadowsky said as he paced. "There was no chance you were supposed to win. There was no chance you were supposed to make the NCAA Tournament; less than no chance that you were going to win the Big Ten [Tournament]"

"This, scoring three goals in the third to tie them, it's improbable. Your whole year has been improbable. That's right up your alley. When the puck drops, go show them."

And then he left the room.

■ ■ ■

Long before Gadowsky ever had to rally the troops he found himself in a much different place as he stood over his first tee shot of the day. The hole in question was a long Par 4 with a patch of pine trees to the right and a formidable bunker to the left. He swung, and then started to lean as the ball zipped through the air.

The shot would bleed right, still managing to avoid the trees and find a slight gap in the wooded area that gave him a short iron to the green. But before he took his second, a voice called out from an elevated tee box nearby. It was a fellow member of Centre Hills Golf Club, a well-wisher giving Gadowsky his best before the upcoming season.

That day, Gadowsky had no inkling the kind of the season his team was about to embark on. In fact, there was every reason to believe Penn State would finally take a step backwards because sports' own laws of physics did not allow for a new program to build so smoothly. In four short years of Division I hockey each season had surpassed the last.

Better players, better results, a better product. Sooner or later, something wouldn't go Penn State's way.

With 11 new faces that included an unproven pair of goalies, this seemed to be the year things would come back down to earth. These Nittany Lion might be the first to make the NCAA Tournament, but it wouldn't be in 2017. Or so everyone thought.

Penn State's chances would boil down to goalkeeping. Peyton Jones, an athlete widely considered to be the best goaltender on the prospect market was set to step in. The only problem was Penn State's coaching staff never planned for Jones to be the primary goalie his freshman year. He would work behind McAdam, pick up a few starts and be far more prepared when his name was called in the years to come.

But with McAdam gone, there were few other options. Career backup goalie Chris Funkey was as respected and as successful as they come, but there was no reason to assume he was the answer. Much of Penn State's early success laid on a host of solid goaltenders, and with that proven commodity gone, the sense of security was replaced with a lingering fear that the program's momentum might leave as quickly as it came.

Close losses were manageable, but uncertainty up and down the roster opened the door to far less comforting possibilities.

With pleasantries exchanged, both golfers were off to find their next shot. "We'll have to see." Gadowsky said, picking his ball out of the hole.

■ ■ ■

By the time Penn State's exhibition game against Ontario-based Queen's University arrived there were more answers than before but not necessarily different expectations.

Having deferred his enrollment for another year, freshman forward Denis Smirnov had been impressive in practice, looking the part of a player a year older and wiser. Andrew Sturtz returned to campus as well, in even better shape than the year prior. If early returns were any indication, the strength and conditioning of the team was a step above the year before, a theme that would not be forgotten later in the season.

Despite an easy 8-0 Penn State exhibition win, it was a crosscheck to star defenseman Kevin Kerr late in the game that was the first potential bad omen of the season. Kerr struggled to leave the ice, and in a meaningless game the Nittany Lions looked to be an MRI away from their first bad news of the year.

Amazingly, though, especially for anyone who saw the hit, Kerr was fine apart from a few bumps and bruises. He didn't even miss Penn State's opening series against No. 16

St Lawrence four days later. Any questions about Kerr's health were quickly forgotten as he went plus-2, helping Penn State upset the Saints. Despite falling behind 1-0 just 7:51 in the game, the Nittany Lions leaned on an energetic crowd and slowly gained their footing. Two minutes later, it was Dylan Richard, whose career is paved with key plays, finding the back of the net as Smirnov picked up his first point on the assist in Hockey

Valley.

From there Penn State largely controlled the flow, and David Thompson made it 2-1 after the first period as the Nittany Lions continued their tradition of pucks on net, out-shooting St Lawrence 16-7.

While one period wouldn't be enough to establish Jones' reputation, a 14-save second period was his first true moment to shine. Penn State made the most of a strong goaltending performance as Stutz collected a shorthanded rebound and to make it 3-1. A Blake Gober empty netter finished off the night at 4-2, as St. Lawrence couldn't follow up on an early third period goal.

The result was a positive one for Penn State, but as the Nittany Lions learned the very next night, they were far from a finished product. That would become readily apparent as St Lawrence scored three goals in the opening five minutes, forcing Gadowsky to pull Jones from the net.

Technically it was a two-goal game after the second period, but the Nittany Lions never really threatened. As the final horn sounded, the coaching staff knew that the 6-3 defeat would be another valuable teaching moment. Inside the locker room the mood was the same. Goodwin was annoyed, fellow veterans equally so, but also aware that a generally inexperienced team was going to go through some growing pains. The important part was to avoid the same mistakes. And until January, many months later, Penn State never found itself in that situation again.

If there was a moment that Penn State's season showed the first signs of something special it came in South Bend, Indiana, just two weeks following that loss to St. Lawrence. Penn State had dispatched Mercyhurst 7-0 the week prior, and then set its sights on the No. 3 Irish. For a team looking to gain experience, it wouldn't get much better than on the road against a Top 5 team.

Penn State opened the series doing what it had done the past four years, outshooting its opponent for much of the night. In an odd statistical twist, Penn State scored two goals on just eight shots in the second period, the only one during which Notre Dame controlled the shot count. By the game's end, it was a 3-3 tie and Penn State headed back to the team hotel satisfied, if not slightly disappointed, that it had come so close to an upset.

Even so, the team had fared well on the biggest stage thus far.

If Friday night was cause for cautious optimism then Saturday night delivered validation when Sturtz scored in transition taking a pass from Smirnov just 1:20 into the overtime.

The win gave Penn State a meaningful, 3-2 victory over a Top 5 team.

A few hundred miles away, Penn State football found itself in a dogfight with Ohio State en route to what would become its own season-defining upset. An anxious crowd got the momentum boost it wanted from an unlikely source when the Beaver Stadium public address announcer gave this news during a timeout:

"A final in overtime, in men's hockey: Penn State 3, Notre Dame 2."

The football crowd roared with satisfaction, and Penn State hockey found itself slowly entering the public consciousness. Back in Indiana on the team plane, video of the Beaver Stadium announcement made its way to the phones of players waiting to fly back to State College. Many had spent their time on the runway keeping tabs on Penn State football's night. When the wheels finally left the ground Ohio State was ahead, and seemed poised to win.

It was their pilot who broke the news of the historic and unexpected upset as Penn State landed back in State College, cheers rippling through the chartered plane. October 22 was a night to remember for Penn State athletics. Football went all the way to a Big Ten title, and hockey won the next eight games, none by fewer than two goals.

For Gadowsky, that success was welcome but it still wasn't an indication Penn State was better than he or his staff had expected. The Nittany Lions had dispatched teams that it should have, scoring seven and eight goals against Division I newcomer Arizona State, blowing by Alaska-Anchorage, Canisius and Niagara. The next test, a Big Ten schedule opening series against Michigan, would define what exactly this team could be. The Wolverines were the perfect litmus test. Michigan was a year removed from the

CCM line, but still boasted a veteran goalie Zach Nagelvoort and plenty of familiar faces. This team wasn't as deadly, but Michigan was still Michigan.

Penn State ran straight through the Wolverines. The first night of the series, the Nittany Lions scored three goals in the second period to go up 4-0 in dominating fashion.

Michigan was fortunate to be down only 4-0 after a 15-8 barrage on goal by Penn State in the opening 20 minutes of play. Liam Folkes scored his second of the year just 4:42 into the middle period and two more goals in the final five minutes of the period to blow the game wide open. Smirnov ended the night with three points and Jones notched his first Big Ten win with 28 saves.

The next night was more of the same, three goals in the opening period by Penn State made it 3-1 after the first. Smirnov added two more points to his total while Penn State outshot Michigan 58-23 in one of the season's most dominating performances, winning 6-1.

Gadowsky found himself reevaluating expectations. Following the game he, Fisher and Lindsay walked in silence down one of the many hallways deep inside the arena. But eventually they confirmed to each other out loud what they all had seen, and what they were all thinking; this team had dominated an established program. The Wolverines were missing some of the players that had made them elite the year prior, but these were convincing wins against a team that had shut out No. 4 Boston University 4-0 three weeks prior.

"We didn't squeak out those wins," Gadowsky would later remark. "Those wins meant something." The Nittany Lions traveled to face Ohio State looking to make good on a big moment. It was probably the best test Penn State could have asked for at that point. The Buckeyes had been a thorn in the Nittany Lions' side over the years, and Ohio State's offense was one of the few that matched Penn State's. This series looked to set the pace in the conference title race.

Penn State didn't know it at the time, but a Friday night 3-0 loss to open the series would be the blueprint for the Nittany Lions' later struggles. Penn State outshot the Buckeyes 46-21, but managed not a single goal as Ohio State slowly accumulated one each period; this even as Penn State managed 17 shots on goal in the third period while holding Ohio State to just three. The Nittany Lions took just one penalty, but went 0-4 on their own power play opportunities. An offense that was essentially the nation's most lethal had no answer to cracking Ohio State goalie Christian Frey, who would mention following the game that like every team that faces Penn State, the Buckeyes had spent the week preparing for a massive shot total and jumping on loose pucks.

The message from Penn State's staff that night was to continue on the same path. The goals would come, and it stood to reason that a 20-plus shot differential would lead to more wins than losses over the course of the season. Saturday night that theory held true, although not as quickly as Gadowsky and company would have liked. It took until 4:16 into the second period for Brandon Biro to break the scoreless tie and give Penn State its first lead of the series. Then just 3:10 into the third period, Erik Autio scored an unassisted tally to push Penn State ahead 2-0.

A shorthanded goal by Ricky DeRosa just five minutes later handed the Nittany Lions a comfortable lead to work with. Ohio State's own explosive offense would get within a goal in the final 10 minutes, but once again Penn State's stifling defense gave Ohio State very few shot opportunities. By the night's end, Penn State had a 89-47 shot advantage in the series and on that night, a 4-2 victory to show for it.

The ensuing week was more of the same, in State College to sweep Michigan State. By the end of the weekend it was two straight offense heavy games for Penn State and in this case a pair of 5-2 and 5-3 victories as a result.

Meanwhile, Penn State continued its steady ascent up the national rankings. The Nittany Lions' success was legitimate, but the program's top 20 ascension was benefitting from turmoil at the top of the rankings. By the time the sweep of Michigan State was complete, Penn State knew that come Monday it might find itself atop the rankings at No.1.

The news broke during a media session with Gadowsky and players a few days prior to a late January home series against Ohio State. The national rankings were released at noon, but delays had reporters feverishly refreshing the USCHO website, waiting for the update as they conducted interviews. When the news finally came, the response was predictable.

"We truly don't follow the polls that much," Gadowsky said. "We don't."

DeRosa took a more honest approach, noting what was undoubtedly true behind closed doors " It's pretty cool." he said with a smile.

If Penn State was taking things in stride, it was safe to say elsewhere the world was turning into a bit of a circus. Football media members turned their attention towards hockey, showing up to cover games. The national hockey media began to dissect Penn State's rise through the ranks, openly questioning the schedule, and in turn, the Nittany Lions' 16-2-1 record. It was a fair debate, but did little to soften the anticipation for the upcoming and hotly contested series against Ohio State for the second time in three weeks.

When Friday finally arrived the atmosphere inside Pegula Ice Arena was a bit different.

In a few short years Penn State hockey had transitioned from a novelty to something fans were genuinely passionate about. This was no longer just a feel-good endeavor. It had reached a new level of emotional investment. Tickets were harder to find, jerseys easier to spot downtown. Fans poured into the building the second the doors opened and brought with them a wave of anticipation. Penn State had, on some level, finally arrived.

In the first period Penn State dominated Ohio State in essentially every facet. James Robinson made the most of the early pressure, scoring 7:48 into the game and blowing the roof off the building in the process. The Nittany Lions would get 24 shots on goal during the opening 20 minutes of play while holding Ohio State to just three on Peyton Jones.

Though fans roared with approval, Penn State found itself only up a goal despite an imposing first period. The small margin turned into a tie game midway through the second, so Vince Pedrie's goal with just under two minutes to go in the period looked to be a crucial moment. Penn State was up 2-1 and rare gave up leads at home, let alone in the third period.

Ohio State didn't care about tendencies, tying the game again just minutes into the final period. And yet the crowd, tense on edge, rose to its feet and erupted as Alec Marsh beat Frey with just over seven minutes to go putting Penn State back up a goal. In the past, Penn State's coaching staff had remarked that the difference between good teams and great ones was a killer instinct. This felt particularly true as Ohio State tied the game at 3-3 just a minute following Marsh's goal. After dominating Ohio State in the first period and holding steady in the second, Penn State found itself in overtime despite a 59-27 shot differential.

Eventually it was Ohio State celebrating with the extra point, having won the shootout at the conclusion of the five minute overtime period. Penn State left the game with a point in the standings, but it was a game that should have been a Nittany Lion victory.

Postgame Gadowsky held true to form, publically not giving too much attention to that No.1 ranking, but the implications were clear. In a town and in an athletic department familiar with high levels of success, the loud buzz surrounding the ranking and the expectations that came with it were influences he had never experienced before. All of Gadowsky's experiences in coaching hadn't really prepared him for the fishbowl.

Attention at Penn State is a very different animal than at Princeton or Alaska Anchorage, and the management of that attention was a maturing skillset.

Reflecting months later, Gadowsky would admit that the ranking should have been handled internally with more purpose, and that the distraction it brought may have been underestimated and underappreciated. In a postseason autopsy, players and coaches likened it to something like arrogance, even if it wasn't intentional. Penn State would win because it was No. 1, and because quite frankly the team hadn't been doing much in the way of losing.

Whatever it might have been, Penn State lost to Ohio State the following night 6-3 in a game that was closer than the final score. It was the opening salvo in what would become a difficult stretch for the Nittany Lions. For this was yet another game Penn State sat on the right end of the shot total by a wide 44-28 margin and failed to get the result. As the buzzer sounded, Ohio State players cheered and not long after a broom would fly through the air and land on the ice. While the tie and the win didn't technically mea a sweep in the standings, Ohio State left State College without losing to nation's newest No. 1 team two nights in a row.

Goodwin and nearly every player would not forget that broom, all fuming following the game and during postgame interview sessions, but neither Goodwin nor his teammates would see the Buckeyes again in 2017. "For some reason, it just felt like we were going for the home-run play all night," Gadowsky said. "We wanted to do something special instead of playing the way we play. I think the effort was there, but the attention to playing together wasn't."

The following weeks appeared to be the end of the road for the Nittany Lions' unexpected rise. A 5-4 loss to Princeton hinged on a controversial goal that began when the puck appeared to leave the ice and hit the netting. Players slowed slightly, expecting a stoppage in play. A whistle never came but the goal did. In Minneapolis, the Gophers rolled over Penn State 5-1 and 5-2 despite a stronger start and a near 2-0 lead for the Nittany Lions on Saturday night. In either regard, it was an eye-opener for a program that thought it had something special in the works.

It was around this time that Gadowsky made an unexpected admission. He needed help.

The team had not responded to the No. 1 ranking as he had hoped or expected. Perhaps it was a result of him not preparing the team, or simply that they had peaked too early.

Whatever the case, something was missing. So Gadowsky turned to a man just a few hundred yards from his own office, asking for just 10 minutes of James Franklin's time. "Once he understood what I wanted, we talked for an hour," Gadowsky recalled about their meeting.

What they discussed in specifics remains a private conversation, even as Gadowsky retold the experience, but the broad strokes focused on the management of outside noise, expectations, and general concepts of compartmentalizing. By the time

Gadowsky left the meeting, he was confident he had the tools to refocus the team and hit the reset button for an important stretch of games. "I'll take that with me forever," Gadowsky said. "I felt far more optimistic after it."

That optimism shined through in a series against Wisconsin. A mid-Feburary night, Penn State rolled past a surging Badger team to the tune of 6-3. The next night it was 5-2, and Penn State was back on track.

But during the bounce back victories, Kevin Kerr suffered a lower body injury. He had dodged a bullet against Queen's, but was not so lucky after taking a bad fall into the boards. Gadowsky reluctantly announced that Kerr was out for the remainder of the season, and with it, Penn State suffered a significant blow to its chances moving forward."I thought that might have been the nail," Gadowsky would later say.

With Kerr out, Penn State would have to rely on freshman Kris Myllari, who had been a consistent presence all season, but in far more supplementary roles. The challenge now was to pick up where Penn State's most talented defenseman had left off, and in this particular case, to do it against Minnesota the upcoming week.

A CHALLENGE

David Goodwin verbally committed to Penn State just days before Bill O'Brien was hired to coach Penn State football. The two had never met, and only one knew the other by name. But they are almost certainly linked. O'Brien took a job with no certain future, even before the NCAA sanctions were handed down.

And Goodwin took a chance on Penn State, too. It was a program that couldn't promise winning while he was on campus. A program with no certain future and a program that was forming in the middle of history's most unprecedented scandal. Nobody would have blamed O'Brien for saying no, and you can say the same for Goodwin, as well.

But they accepted the challenge, and in their own way both continued a building process.

For Goodwin and his teammates, the risk they were taking was much larger than the coach's. If O'Brien failed he would leave Penn State with millions and another job waiting for him at nearly any level of the sport. Penn State hockey players, however, already faced a challenge simply to be one of the few to go to the professional ranks. Adding in the unknowns of Penn State's future and the risk of that damaging their personal athletic career, their risk became even greater.

However, to know David Goodwin is to know someone who is not afraid of a challenge, putting in the hard work and the long hours. It's an interesting juxtaposition of his personality. He is light-hearted and funny, but underneath the surface a far more serious person.

Take, for example, the 2015 season. As Penn State headed into a crucial series against Wisconsin, a tweet flashed across Goodwin's screen. It showed where Penn State would stand in the postseason race if it won and where it would fall in the wake of defeat. A win would further their case, a loss would likely end it.

Penn State lost the series.

And Goodwin saved the tweet.

A screenshot sat on his camera roll for over a year until the two teams met again. The first night of the series Goodwin scored just over six minutes into the game, and Penn State won 6-3. The next night 5-2. The Nittany Lions were the better team heading into that series, but it was hard to ignore the edge and even harder to not notice who scored that tone-setter of a first goal; especially after 2015, when the Nittany Lions got so close to the postseason, only to fall short.

That was what made Goodwin such a good captain in Penn State's historic season. He was never the flashiest or the best at any one thing, but he was never outworked, and he rarely relented.

To know David Goodwin is also to know what it means to see more than hockey. In the summer of 2015 Goodwin, a Spanish major, traveled to Mexico to study Spanish culture and continue to strengthen his understanding of the language.

"I stayed with a Mexican family who was only able to speak Spanish," said Goodwin. "It's a little bit different from other programs where you get to stay in an apartment or a dorm. I really thought that staying with a Spanish speaking family would be the best for me to immerse myself in the culture and in the language."

A year later, he traveled to Cuba and taught English at a local university, serving in the community as he worked on local projects and made friends all the while. In the last moments of free time before his senior season, Goodwin was giving back to a culture that had become a part of him.

"I think just the awareness of how other people live in the world, experiencing that there's way more to life than the material things, there's way more to life than hockey," Goodwin said. "To see the joys the families had in each other and spending time with each other was something that I felt had been lacking in my life in America. So just bringing back that joy and appreciation for the smaller things in life I think Americans take for granted."

Which is why it made sense that he was named captain of Penn State's 2016-17 team. If anyone was about the greater good it was him. If anyone was about putting in the extra effort it was him.

"David Goodwin has always been a highly intelligent player who has consistently generated offense on whatever line he has played on," Gadowsky said. "Equally impressive is that David has worked extremely hard to improve his individual battles to become one of the team's top performers in that area."

Early in his career Goodwin had played alongside Casey Bailey and Taylor Holstrom, the latter a huge influence in his career. The three would become one of the most dominant lines in the Big Ten, and in turn, Goodwin's stats would continue to rise.

Then Bailey headed to the NHL.

And then Holstrom graduated.

All that was left was Goodwin, and the biggest challenge of all. Could he do it on his own?

The results speak for themselves. Under Goodwin's guidance Penn State had the best season in the program's short history. Goodwin was no small part of that success, playing in all 39 games while racking up 38 points, second best on the team behind his Russian counterpart and fellow forward Denis Smirnov.

So everyone had their answer. Just as there was more to Goodwin than hockey, there was more to his hockey than simply being part of a line. But the ride had to end eventually, and as Denver skated into the Frozen Four, Goodwin's eyes welled up with tears as he addressed his teammates in the locker room, still wearing his uniform.

"We should be really proud of what we accomplished," he said, running his hands through his hair. "I'm going to look back on this year with so much pride. I can't wait to see what you guys do in the future." What that future holds is unknown. Like O'Brien he leaves Penn State in a better place than he found it, and will head to Finland to continue his playing career.

And to know Goodwin is to know what built Penn State hockey in the first place: players who took a chance on a program that could make them no promises. Instead, those players took that program, made promises to give it everything they had, and built it into a rising power of the sport.

ARRIVAL

2016-17
Pt 2

The stakes couldn't have been higher as both teams hit the ice February 17 at Pegula. Penn State was just on the outside of the Big Ten title race and quickly slipping towards the NCAA Tournament bubble. There was no time to be learning lessons sometime down the road.

Minnesota was not only exceptionally talented, but the Gophers had dismissed and disliked Penn State hockey from the outset. Minnesota's coaching staff was the only one to turn down postgame interviews in Penn State's media room, allegedly to avoid the Penn State branding behind them. Players have enjoyed victories and fans have been some of the most vocal about their dislike of Penn State's impact on the college hockey landscape.

So on Friday night all of that and more was in play with the Gophers just a few wins from locking up a regular season title, while Penn State could secure its first-ever postseason berth.

Minnesota scored first, but the lead was short-lived as Sturtz tied the game just 8:50 into the contest. It was a period reminiscent of the dominance against Ohio State weeks earlier with Penn State boasting a 15-8 shot advantage. But in this case, no lead at the intermission. Twenty minutes later, Minnesota carried a 3-2 lead into the third period. Myllari made the most of his increased role, tying the game, but Minnesota added two more in the final minutes to seal it.

One night down, and a 6-3 defeat to show for it. The coaching staff stayed confident. Their team had played well for 60 minutes but simply got beat. Forty-three shots on goal was a performance the team could live with, but the late powerplay goal was a mistake to be remedied. So they would stay the course.

On Saturday, night the intensity and the stakes were and even greater. If Penn State hockey was going to make the NCAA Tournament, it could happen in the next few hours. Fans were living and dying on each shot and pass. It wasn't the playoffs, but it sure felt like it.

Penn State struck fast as Smirnov scored just 3:17 into the game and the Nittany Lions' defense shut out the Gophers for the first period. Twenty minutes in the books, 40 to go for history. Then Goodwin made it 2-0 as Penn State continued to pound the puck on goal. In total, Penn State would finish the night with 45 shots to Minnesota's 29. The game sat at 2-0 after two periods.

But as everyone in the building knew, Minnesota was far too good to assume the Gophers were down and out. Their fear was confirmed as Minnesota tied the game at 2-2, and the crowd went silent. With just under two minutes play it looked as though destiny had come calling. Smirnov, who had become one of the best freshmen in the entire country, went hard to the net with the puck and was taken down from behind. The crowd was livid, and slowly but surely the referee pointed to the center of the ice. A penalty shot awaited.

Penn State had struggled at shootouts in the past. Ironically enough, if the Nittany Lions were going to punch an NCAA ticket that night, it would have to come from the one thing an explosive team wasn't particularly good at.

Penn State's bench was in a brief panic. Smirnov had just skated the length of the ice, and now would have to do it again, with the season on the end of his stick. Gadowsky offered to call a timeout to give his freshman a chance to rest, but Smirnov waved him off. By the time Smirnov got to the puck at center ice, a packed rink of just over 6,100 was silent. As he skated down the ice somehow it got even quieter. The seven seconds it took him to cover the length of the ice felt like seven hours for each and every fan in the building.

But as he calmly slipped the puck between the legs of Eric Schierhorn and into the back of the net, the building erupted with the loudest cheer in the short history of the program. The metal rafters shook, the glass rattled and Smirnov jumped straight into his teammates' arms on the bench. Pandemonium at the rink. For the next minute and a half the crowd roared each time Penn State cleared the puck out of the defensive zone. The job seemed all but complete with four seconds remaining as the teams prepared for a faceoff in Penn State's zone.

Later Gadowsky would say that his players did their job, but the one thing that could happen, did. Justin Kloos got the puck off the draw and fired it just under the crossbar past Jones with three seconds to play. The tie game crushed Penn State's bench and sent the crowd into a very different kind of silence.

The game went go to overtime, and the heartbreak was total as Rem Pitlick beat Jones for the game winner three minutes later.

A shell-shocked Penn State team skated off the ice as Minnesota celebrated its improbable win. The Gophers had been taken to task and and yet somehow sat at the end of the weekend with two wins and in the driver's seat for the Big Ten Title.

After the fact, it was a matter of damage control. Heartbreaking losses late in the season can linger in the psyche of a team for far longer than usual. Gadowsky and his players insisted that it wouldn't happen, but the concern amongst the coaching staff was real.

"That's the type of game you're going to see in the Big Ten Tournament," Gadowsky said as he paced the locker room. "And if you get your heads up and look at it and how we get this much better you're going to be a lot better for it. And the next time around we're going to win that fucker."

Down the hallway and hours later, Gadowsky was still troubled by the tying goal. And so he sent film of the last-second faceoff to Dallas Stars' coach Ken Hitchcock. The two had become close during Gadowsky's stay at Princeton thanks to an odd twist of fate. At the time Gadowsky's staff was looking for a little extra help, and so on whim he called Hitchcock, then head coach of the Philadelphia Flyers to see if he had any staff to spare as the NHL waded through its lockout.

"What if I came down?" Hitchcock said, he too without much to do, unable to legally work with his current team.

And so Hitchcock did. The first time to a throng of media members; the result of which was Hitchcock sneaking into subsequent practices to avoid detection, advising almost quite literally in secret. When Princeton was on the road, Hitchcock would receive game tape and review it, offering up his insight just days later.

"I thought he'd be here for a week, and he was there the entire year," Gadowsky said. "He'd go to at least one of our games a week, usually two. If he couldn't make an away game, we'd send him the tapes. If I had any questions he'd come in hours before practice and just sit there. I'd shut the door and take the phone off the hook and just ask him every little question. It was an amazing learning experience as a young coach. It was phenomenal."

In the wake of a defeat Gadowsky felt partially responsible for, he needed that guidance again.

"Guy has become a tremendous student of the game," Hitchcock said years earlier. "His best attribute is that he asks for help and asks the tough questions to get to the next level as a coach."

With the Penn State film in his inbox, Hitchcock offered up his thoughts the very next day.

It was also a moment that would define Penn State in another way. The feeling inside the program was that Penn State had played well enough to win on two different occasions and had twice come away with late defeats. As the Big Ten Tournament closed in, even if it meant a harder road, coaches and players hoped for one final shot at the Gophers.

"It would be nice." Sturtz would say with a smile.

But in the immediate future Penn State still had work to do. Two solid 4-2 and 4-1 victories at Michigan State later, Penn State had won both of its must-have games to keep NCAA Tournament hopes alive.

Back in State College, it was a fairly straightforward task for Penn State. A win against Wisconsin would be a major step in locking up a tournament bid, or at least continue to increase those odds. But the Badgers leaned on a newfound offensive attack, beating Penn State 7-4 thanks to two three-goal periods, scoring twice in the final six minutes to blow the game wide open. It was a bit of shock to the system for a Penn State, and it stood to reason that Senior Night would be a different story.

And the 6-0 rout was. The Nittany Lions scored twice in the first period, as Myllari continued his strong play in relief of Kerr, and Goodwin added one of his own. David Thompson scored midway through the second to extend the lead, while Peyton Jones put up a 36-save shutout effort.

In a fitting conclusion, Penn State put all five seniors out on the ice for a final minute powerplay, a unit so hilarious in its concept that tough-man forward Zach Saar found himself playing as a defenseman for the first time in his career. It was a move he enjoyed all the more in his final game at Pegula, as he blasted home a goal in the final seconds, the bench nearly clearing with excitement in the process.

Weeks after a loss that could have ended the season, it was all smiles on a bench that had looked so defeated. Locked in to the No. 9 spot in the PairWise rankings, the postseason seemed all but guaranteed. But then the Nittany Lions traveled to Michigan to close out the season and managed just two goals in the series. In legendary coach Red Berenson's final game on the bench in Ann Arbor, Penn State lost 3-2 on Friday night despite a 37-17 shot total and thanks in large part to the heroic goaltending of Hayden Lavigne.

On Saturday night, Penn State had two first-period goals waved off as Michigan was content to repeatedly clear the puck and play prevent defense. Penn State would give up four goals, falling 4-0 despite a whopping 46-23 shot differential. After the game, Gadowsky approached Jones in the locker room, an unusual for both parties. The conversation was brief but important to setting the table the next week. Gadowsky emphasized that Jones was Penn State's goalie, and even after a rough series the Nittany Lions would need him in the Big Ten Tournament. A vote of confidence.

Penn State's fourth place finish in the Big Ten would mean that the Nittany Lions were set to face Michigan again in the first round of the conference tournament in Detroit. Perhaps a neutral site would tilt things back in Penn State's favor. With that in mind, Penn State set its sights on the potential second-round meeting with the Gophers -albeit privately- awaiting the winner of Penn State/Michigan. A chance for redemption after heartbreak.

"We were confident." Gadowsky said.

Travel to Detroit wasn't easy. Penn State's plane failed to land in State College due to extreme wind passing through the area. As a result, Penn State loaded a bus and drove to Detroit. One long night with a nearly $600 stop at an innocent Chipotle near the Ohio border later, Penn State found itself less than 24 hours from a tournament to define the season.

To the surprise of no one, perhaps not even Michigan, Penn State came out swinging and dominated the Wolverines. With the Nittany Lions leading 3-0 at the first intermission, the victory seemed to be a foregone conclusion and Michigan's third period indifference made for a fairly drama-free opening round victory. In the week leading up to the Big Ten Tournament, the talk had been two-fold. Penn State was a win away from the NCAA Tournament. But Penn State was also a win away from something much more emotionally meaningful: a date with Minnesota for the fifth time.

"We wanted to beat them." Gadowsky later admitted. It wasn't about the Big Ten Tournament. It wasn't even about the NCAA Tournament. It was one thing and one thing only. Minnesota. This was most evident as Gadowsky stood in front of his team minutes before they hit the ice.

"Can I tell you my feelings, are you cool with that?" Gadowsky said with his patented grin, fiddling with a ball of tape in his hand as his team looked on.

"So this game, what you're playing for is a trip to the Big Ten Championship," he said as he started to walk. "For the program, that would mean a great deal. Telling you my feelings? That would mean a great deal, too. It also would basically guarantee you guys would be going to the NCAA Tournament. That also would be huge for the program and since I'm telling you my feelings, I think that would be extremely cool and would mean a ton to me, too."

But then Gadowsky went quiet, and his tone changed. Suddenly he too remembered that last-second heartbreak to Minnesota, or perhaps he had never stopped thinking about it.

"With that being the case, I've got to honest with you. All I can think of right now is how bad I want to beat that team," Gadowsky said, his voice cracking, pointing towards the door where the Gophers lay in wait. "So please go ahead and do that, alright?"

Nikita Pavlychev's goal just 1:05 into the game as he pounded away in front of the net represented more than a little pent up animosity. Minnesota took it in stride, the Gophers eventually going up 2-1 after the first period.

So the dogfight was on.

Less than four minutes into the second period Alec Marsh scored to tie the game for the middle period's only goal. Penn State had rifled 16 shots at Eric Schierhorn in the second period and constantly appeared just one bounce from taking the lead. That bounce finally came when Dylan Richard added to his laundry list of big moments and gave Penn State a 3-2 lead. It was a short-lived luxury as Minnesota tied the game yet again just two minutes later.

For all of the talk about Penn State's offense during its quick rise through the rankings during this season, it was Peyton Jones who had perhaps lived up to the hype most of all. Jones made 40 saves that night, including a few of the career-highlight-reel variety. Teammates would compare Jones' calm demeanor and play throughout the season to Montréal Canadian netminder Carey Price.

Neither team broke through during the first overtime and the game found itself headed to a second overtime. The mood in the locker room was light, and it was DeRosa who made a prophetic declaration that it might be the team's quietest player who would find the winner.

"I think the Fin has got it," DeRosa said of defenseman Erik Autio.

Autio, a soft-spoken but immensely reliable defenseman had become a backbone for Penn State's defensive corps alongside a physical Pedrie. Autio's reliability was on display moments before, diving to stop a near-breakaway attempt by Minnesota that could have turned the game into the fifth heartbreak of the season.

And then it finally happened. Just moments after his defensive game-saver, Autio trailed the offensive attack as Smirnov worked along the right boards and nearly behind the goal. At the last second Smirnov saw his European brother-in-arms, cleanly passing the puck through traffic to Autio who, with 13:33 gone by in the second overtime, directed the puck into a wide-open net.

The ensuing celebration was about as euphoric as they come. Players joyfully rushed the ice, knowing they were headed to the NCAA Tournament, and they had at last slayed their dragon.

It was hard to know what to expect from Penn State in the Big Ten Tournament title game against Wisconsin the next night. While the Nittany Lions stood firmly in the NCAA Tournament picture, Wisconsin needed a win to lock up a bid. If nothing else, it was a matter of each team's fitness. Penn State was about to enter what amounted to its fourth game in three days, whereas Wisconsin had enjoyed the benefits of a first round bye and a fairly simple victory over Michigan State to make the title game.

It was hard to imagine Penn State having the emotional interest and investment, let alone the physical strength to get through another game. Gadowsky's pregame speech was simply two silent laps around the locker room as his team looked on. Then he headed towards the door, handing Funkey the lineup card, and then he and the staff left the room to cheers as the unspoken speech concluded.

If Wisconsin had scored first the Nittany Lions might have folded, but Liam Folkes scored late in the first period and Penn State found itself up 1-0 in the conference championship. The Nittany Lions were playing tired, but they weren't about to quit now.

The feeling in the locker room was positive, but the coaching staff was not so secretly leery that the legs could quite literally fall off at any moment. Even so, the decision was the same it had been all year, keep shooting the puck. "That was center bar," Gadowsky said to the locker room about Folkes' goal. "If I was you I would fucking shoot it in the middle of the net every time, nice shot. "Nice shot but I'm just saying."

In the second period, Penn State continued to hang on to the slim lead, and after 40 minutes the shot count was limited to just 32 shots between the two teams. Jones was particularly sharp for the third straight night. Players and coaches would later mention --unprompted-- that Jones' performance was one of the best three-day spans that they had ever seen by a goalie.

Wisconsin's urgency finally overcame Penn State's tired legs as the Badgers fired 18 shots and tied the game at 1-1 on a power play. Somehow, Penn State had managed to take the game and the weekend to another overtime period.

"I don't care if it takes five minutes or four periods, we're winning the hockey game," DeRosa told his teammates during the intermission, making what would be his second proclamation in as many days.

"If you guys were writing this story, it would sound way better in overtime anyway," Gadowsky added. "But I'm hungry so let's win this."

As Wisconsin headed to the power play with just under five minutes to go in the first overtime, it appeared to be the moment Penn State would finally succumb to its own exhaustion.

But it never happened. Jones continued to stand on his head, and Penn State survived the shorthanded sequence and the first overtime. As the teams headed to the locker room, pizza found its way there as well. Gadowsky dove in for a slice, remarking as he did that if there ever was a team to win a game like this, against all odds, it was this one. "Fucking playing in their end, fire pucks, get to the net, and win the game," he said leaving the room with slice in hand.

In spite of everything, in spite of exhaustion, in spite of Minnesota and in spite of all the obstacles, Penn State won. Just 6:43 into the second overtime Liam Folkes took a pass from Brandon Biro as he flew down the ice on a breakaway. A subtle shoulder move and stick fake later, the puck was in the net. And the Big Ten Championship was theirs.

The ensuing celebration was the thing of movies. Players clambered over the bench to get to Folkes, who raced around the ice with no predetermined destination. Sturtz turned to Gadowsky on the bench and joined his coaching staff in a long joyous embrace. This moment was something they had all dreamed of, but they never truly knew when it would arrive. Penn State was Big Ten Tournament Champion. There was a banner to be raised and the NCAA Tournament was officially a lock.

There was a little sleep for a team that needed so much of it. The flight home was a deluge of laughs and smiles, the tweets poured in and the congratulations with them. Folkes heard from

Penn State running back Saquon Barkley who also wears the No. 26 congratulating him on representing the number well. By the time Penn State landed back to State College, it was nearly 4 a.m., but it may as well have been 4p.m., the energy continuing to flow through the bus back to campus.

Hours later, the team slowly filed into the basement of Lettermans' outside of downtown State College to find out their fate for the NCAA Tournament. There were still plenty of smiles, but the week had finally caught up to the team. Pedrie sat at a table with coffee in hand, staring somewhat blankly into space. Jones and Folkes sat together, both devouring a plate of breadsticks and whatever food they could get their hands on.

Penn State was praying for a Saturday game. The tournament began on Friday at some regional sites, but the Nittany Lions were going to need every bit of rest and recovery to get their legs back under them. Strength and conditioning coach Cam Davidson had planned out practice and recovery schedules for each option, but Saturday was a far better day.

Penn State once again got a friendly bounce. The Nittany Lions were scheduled to face Union on Saturday in Cincinnati, the second game of the day at US Bank Arena. A day earlier and Penn State may not have had the legs to compete. That week, the team hardly had the legs to practice.

Coaches and players all noted that the practices leading up to Saturday's game were as bad as any they had all season.

By the time the team reached Cincinnati, a Friday night practice was far better. The ice however, not so much. Players across the roster had their skates recut to be able to hang on an ice surface that was a bit subpar. In point of fact, US Bank Arena is an odd building all its own, sandwiched along the bank of the Ohio River and directly next to Red's Stadium, the building harkening back to

80's style gymnasiums. The concourse is a maze of cracked concrete seemingly glued back together to keep the building standing. Much of the upper deck was covered in tarps and most of the rafters covered in bird nests, tied together with the smell of mothballs.

None of this much mattered to Penn State. As the bus arrived the day of the game there were more smiles than anything else. The Nittany Lions had made it. But as Denver rolled past Michigan Tech, those smiles turned to focused faces as Penn State players sat sprinkled throughout the seating area taping sticks or simply watching the game unfold. By the time the third period began, the Nittany Lions had vanished to the hallways to take part in their usual pregame soccer kick before dressing.

When the ice surface was cleaned and Penn State was set to take the ice, the entire team paced back and forth inside a tight tunnel leading out to the bench. Trevor Hamilton kissed his family, Jones stared down the tunnel, and Goodwin looked back at the student photographer who had snuck into the moment. Cheers rained down from a sizable Penn State contingent that had made the drive to watch history.

It was about to happen.

As the pomp and circumstance finally ended and the puck finally dropped, it took Penn State over 11 minutes to break the scoreless tie, and with it a swell of confidence swept over a pro-Penn State crowd. The Dutchmen were the favorites, but the Nittany Lions had a history of disregarding those sort of facts, and a goal in the postseason was not only historic, but proof that Penn State belonged.

The momentum was short-lived, as Union got the goal right back just a minute later. But then Sturtz retook the lead moments later. Union's Spencer Foo tied the game not long thereafter and both teams appeared to drop all pretense of a traditional feeling-out period in the postseason.

These teams came out swinging with goals in both directions. Myllari confirmed it in the second period as he pushed Penn State ahead 3-2. It would take Union nearly six minutes to tie the game again.

Even after the fact nobody can really explain how it happened, but Penn State took off, one of the nation's most explosive offenses just evaporating a Union defense for two quick goals to end the period. The Nittany Lions got scores from Berger and Richard to make it 5-3 after two periods.

"Five goals on 20 shots," Gadowsky said after the period. "That means we're scoring 25 percent of the time. That means one out of every four shots is a goal. So if one of you guys goes and gets four shots this period, that means you've got a goal. It's not just shooting the puck. It's hitting the net. I'll tell you what, you guys are fresh, I'll bet on your every time. Ok? Let's do it."

As it turned out, those numbers were a bit off. In the third period, Penn State fired off 13 shots, resulting in five goals. It was Nate Sucese a minute into the period, then Smirnov five minutes later ripping a shot just below the bar. Up high in the building Flyers general manager Ron Hextall, who was there to see Union forward Mike Vecchione play, flipped over his lineup card to see Smirnov's numbers.

Penn State would do it all that period. Sturtz added a short-handed goal, Nikita Pavlychev a power play tally. Penn State's coaches didn't know what to say. "We weren't sure," Gadowsky later remarked. "You never plan for this kind of thing. What do you say? Just make sure the celebrations are polite. I still look at the bracket now and see 10-3 and do a double take to see who it was that scored 10 goals."

By the time the game actually ended, it had been over for a while. Penn State left the ice with a 10-3 victory, maybe the most unexpected performance in the tournament's history. If Penn State was going to face the nation's No.1 team and No.1 overall seed, now seemed like a good time indeed.

Of course, the hard truth was that Penn State had its hands full. Denver brought the deepest and most talented team that the program had ever faced. Michigan had the CCM line, Minnesota was a challenge and a one-time meeting with Boston College had proven difficult, but this team was different. But, the odds hadn't mattered much before.

"I have two things," Gadowsky said prior to the game as he paced the locker room. "One is, it is really fun to watch you guys playing Penn State hockey. And two, it's a blast watching you win."

Denver scored twice in the opening seven minutes to put the Nittany Lions on the ropes. The Pioneers were stronger, faster and more talented. Everything Penn State had done well all year Denver was doing better. Not only was Denver a talented team offensively, they were one of the nation's best on defense.

Then Pavylchev scored on a roaring shorthanded chance late in the first period proving that the Nittany Lions weren't out of the game just yet. That feeling only grew when just 2:02 into the second period, Smirnov tied the game and a pro-Penn State crowd awakened.

Penn State nearly took the lead with a two separate odd-man rushes, but it was Denver's scoring moments into a power play that gave the No.1 seed a crucial 3-2 lead and the momentum. Penn State would hang on, but two Pioneer goals in the final five minutes of the period turned it to a 5-2 margin after 40 minutes. And that was when Gadowsky walked into the locker room, scratching his head and searching for the right words.

But they weren't quite enough.

At some point, the ride was always going to end. In this case the 2016-17 edition of Penn State hockey found its final moments on March 26. The Nittany Lions would pull within two goals with eight minutes to play, but an empty net goal prevented any true comeback attempt. Denver was the better team, and beyond the admirable fight the Nittany Lions had put up, there was little reason to doubt the eventual conclusion.

Penn State players entered the locker room and thanked their senior teammates who had paved the way. David Goodwin addressed his teammates with tears in his eyes, and the always-stoic Richard took the podium after the game with a glazed look on his face, still digesting the end of an emotional season.

The rest was a bittersweet celebration by returning players and coaches. Gadowsky lamented that Penn State played Denver after such a difficult two weeks, but acknowledged that was the nature of the postseason challenge. "It was a wake-up call," Gadowsky said. "Just how far we have to go as a team and as coaches."

As fans left the arena, they did so knowing that a decade ago moments like these had been nothing but dreams. The pain of a postseason defeat was a luxury few had ever even imagined coming true. It was fitting, too, that this all happened in a building that wasn't too much unlike Greenberg, where PSU hockey was born; a place where things were slightly outdated and more than a little behind the times.

The flashy lights of Pegula serve their purpose, but that day wasn't about the glitz and glamor.

There would be other chances, and other seasons. It was about arrival, and arriving on a stage that had once seemed so impossible, and even five years earlier, so far away.

THE FUTURE

A whiteboard on the wall next to Gadowsky's desk is full to the edges with notes, lists, tactics and small reminders. It's early May, a few months removed from Penn State's historic season and the dead of offseason.

But a season never really ends, does it?

Earlier in the week, Gadowsky hosted a recruit, and afterwards helped with interviews on the search committee for a new women's hockey coach. (Penn State eventually settled on a former co-worker in Princeton women's coach Jeff Kampersal.) There was a little bit of everything to take care of, little rest after a historic season.

Down the hall, incoming freshman Evan Barratt was getting his bearings. A few days later Barratt would go 70th overall in the NHL Entry Draft to the Chicago Blackhawks.

He would be one of four players with Penn State ties to hear their name called during the draft, a historic weekend in its own right for the PSU program.

Penn State's appearance in the NCAA Tournament was always understood to be a goal and the only question left was when.

Millions of dollars and hundreds of sleepless nights were never going to be for nothing, but the Nittany Lions' success was hardly predetermined although certainly anticipated, expected, and anxiously awaited.

In 2018, the Nittany Lions should be as talented as ever. The roster faces minimal turnover, with the biggest names and faces returning to the ice. This team should be even better, the overall talent continuing to rise year after year.

The pressure will also ratchet up. Penn State is hosting a regional site in Allentown for the 2018 and 2019 NCAA Tournament. A fan favorite with sellout crowds almost a guarantee, the Nittany Lions would be two wins from the Frozen Four; a gift-wrapped opportunity to take that next step, a goal that seemed so ethereal not long ago when players first skated at Pegula.

In many respects, the Frozen Four and the assumption Penn State will make the tournament again in the upcoming season are thoughts Gadowsky doesn't want to contemplate. Leaning back in his chair with a bottle of water in his hands, he delivers a hard truth:

"We finished fourth in a conference of six teams," he says with a smile.

"There is work left to be done."

It won't be getting any easier. 2017 Frozen Four participant Notre Dame joins the fold this season, doing little to water down the weekly competition. The Big Ten Tournament now works as a best-of-three format with the higher seed hosting and the championship determined by a single game. It will elongate the season, but provide teams and fans with far less travel and a far better environment after years of empty-seat championships in Chicago and Detroit.

But for a few moments the program is savoring how far it has come. It wasn't long ago the dream and the program were simply that, just a dream.

Behind the scenes Penn State has become a blueprint to funding a budding college hockey program. While the Pegulas' gift took care of many of those early hurdles, Penn State has maintained its claim as one of just three athletic programs on campus to generate a positive cash flow. Previously, only football and men's basketball, backed by television contracts, held that honor.

Hockey has been a unique money maker in that regard. The Nittany Lions are set to bring in around $2 million in ticket sales alone per season with the increase in single game ticket prices.

In the fiscal year 2016, Penn State men's hockey generated just over $4.3 million in operating revenue, third highest behind football and men's basketball. Impressively, and more to the point of local interest, the program brings in more revenue from ticket sales alone than baseball, men's basketball, and wrestling combined. It's a far cry from that letter some 100 years prior rattling off all the reasons why a hockey program at Penn State would never work.

The future of Penn State hockey, like any sport, is an uncertainty. But for a few short months the Nittany Lions sat in a rarified place, a place where goals had been achieved and a vision was brought to life. A few weeks before the 2017-18 season opener the NHL Network replayed an Islanders and Rangers preseason game with McAdam and Bailey both on the ice. Not long ago that seemed like an impossible milestone.

Penn State may never win a national title or it might become the winningest program in the sport's history. Whatever the case might be, as the leaves change and the summer colors fade, hockey was in the valley and the dream had become reality.

And for so many, that was the biggest victory of all.

AUTHOR'S NOTE

I started blogging about sports over the summer early in college as an excuse to channel some excess energy.

For the most part, I wrote live accounts of games in real time: the Penguins/Red Wings Stanley Cup Final was one of the first things I tried. I remember the rush of excitement as I saw my views hit double digits over the span of the week. I was a drop in an endless ocean, but it was fun all the same.

In truth I never thought I'd get into this line of work. My degree is in political science but despite my love for politics I'm not sure I knew exactly what I was going to do with that degree. Through all of the ups and downs of college I found my way to where I am today.

Taking an unconventional path makes you appreciate the people who have helped get you to the other end all the more. So I would be remiss if I didn't thank a few people and think fondly of a few more:

My parents, for knowing this is what I should be doing. My brother for caring even though he --at best-- just tolerates sports.

Mike Poorman for being there when I've needed it, making me think, and not letting me settle to the easy way out. To Ryan Jones who jokingly but yet inspiringly told me over lunch a year ago that people write bad books all the time so I can too. To Scott Van Pelt for calling up my house in 2011 and deciding that I was somehow qualified to inform people about the news. To John Buccigross for saying yes. To Eric Leighton for giving me a good rate on the cover. To Guy Gadowsky who opened his program up to me and was honest no matter the question.

And to you, the reader, who in some form or another supported me along the way. I imagine some day in the not so distant future I will read passages of this book and think of better ways to say things.

But for now, this is a good benchmark of where I am and something I've proud of having created and thankful to be able to share. And in the end that's all I can ask for.

Ben Jones October 2017

www.ingramcontent.com/pod-product-compliance
Lightning Source LLC
Chambersburg PA
CBHW032134040426
42449CB00005B/239